BIBLE IMPACT

Relationship-Building Studies for Youth

BOOK 1

Edited by Thomas A. Nummela

CPH
SAINT LOUIS

Consultants
William Ameiss, Kurt Bickel, Greg Mueller, Cynthia Wheeler

Contributors
William Ameiss, Beth Blazar, Kurt Bickel, Thomas Couser, Thomas Doyle, Dennis Durham, Timothy Frusti, Richard Gutekunst, Barrie Henke, Sally Hiller, Marty Meyer, Patra Pfotenhauer, Ron Roma, Donna Streufert, Cynthia Wheeler, and John Williams

Erlynne A. Bratvogel, editorial assistant

Your comments and suggestions concerning the material are appreciated. Please write to Product Manager, Youth and Adult Bible Studies, Concordia Publishing House, 3558 S. Jefferson Avenue, St. Louis, MO 63118-3968.

4 5 6 7 8 9 10 11 12 13 07 06 05 04 03 02 01 00 99 98

Contents

Introduction

Welcome to the Bible Impact Series!

Welcome to *Bible Impact!* Each of the eight books in the series will bring 16 more "high impact" studies on the topics your young people want and need to talk about—each one grounded in God's Word.

The topics are "high impact" topics that young Christians face in their daily lives.

The process is "high impact" in that it mixes the study of Scripture with group interaction and discussion in a way that will appeal to young people. As they study God's Word in each session, students will also grow in their relationship with their Lord and Savior, knowing His forgiveness and relying on His love.

The leaders material is written for "high impact" in the classroom. Each lesson is fully and clearly described to ensure success for the leader. Additional pages include tips and techniques to help the leader prepare and lead effective youth Bible classes. (See "Tips for Leaders of Youth Bible Studies" at the close of this book.)

And finally, **the power of the Gospel,** which is at the core of each study, will provide "high impact" on the spiritual lives of the participants in each study.

Your comments are welcome and will "impact" future books in the series.

May God bless your studies so that they have great *impact* for Him!

Tom Nummela, DCE
Youth Curriculum Editor

About This Book

The Studies

The Bible Impact Series is written specifically for high school students, especially those in 9th and 10th grades. The studies will also work with students both younger and older, depending on the topic and the characteristics of the group.

Each of the 16 studies in this book is a complete unit. The studies can be used in any order and in a variety of settings.

The studies are designed for the typical one-hour Sunday morning Bible class. Some congregations may also find them appropriate for other applications: youth Bible studies during the week or topics at youth meetings. They can be expanded or shortened to suit your needs.

Selected studies could also form the core study material for a youth retreat (see the information on the topical index below) or for combined sessions with young people and their parents.

Each study consists of four pages. The last page in each study is a copy-ready Student Page, which you may reproduce for each of your students.

The Leaders Guide pages are integral to each study. They contain a description of the process that will fulfill the objectives for the study. Often important sections of the lesson may be described *only* in the Leaders Guide pages.

For situations where copies are not easily obtained, a convenient and inexpensive set of the Student Pages can be purchased for each student (Bible Impact, Book 1, Student Pages stock number 20-2630). These Student Page sets cannot be used without the Leaders Guide.

Where We're Heading gives a summary of the topic and how God's grace and power will be applied in the study.

The *Objectives* provide the leader with clear goals to keep in mind as the study progresses.

The *Lesson Outline* provides a quick overview of the study: its progression, suggested schedule, and necessary materials. Bibles, pencils, and copies of the Student Page will be needed for every study.

The *Lesson Activities* provide a variety of options for study and discussion. In each study, specific parts of the lesson are designed for small-group discussion. In larger groups, the studies recommend creating small clusters of three to eight students. This allows young people to be resources to each other, to share their feelings and concerns, and to communicate their understandings about God and His Word with each other. This process will help build students' relationships with their Lord, with the leader, and with each other.

This small-group process is integral to the material. Some congregations may have only enough students for a single group. Leaders of these groups are asked to forgive and ignore the frequent references to the small-group process.

Other congregations, though they have larger Bible classes, may be tempted to skip the "small group" steps as unnecessary or complicated. This is not the case. The learning environment will be enhanced as young people are given the opportunity to ask questions, express attitudes, and voice concerns—and are challenged to articulate their faith response in a peer group with whom they are comfortable. (For more information on this subject, an article on adolescent spirituality is summarized in "Tips for Leaders of Youth Bible Studies".)

Also included in this book are helpful tools for the Bible study leader:

1. A *topical index* and a *scriptural index* provide access to these studies in unique ways. While the studies are not directly interrelated, a leader can use these indexes to create small units of similar topics or studies from a single book of the Bible.

For example, a series on personal improvement could include the following studies: "A New Start" (1), "Self-Esteem" (6), Shame on You" (2), and "Surprise Your Family" (3). "Risk Taking" (10), "Suicide" (11), and "Grief" (4) could anchor a series on facing death.

The theme "Caring for Others" is explored in "Homosexuality" (5), Prejudice (7), "AIDS"

(8), and "Ecology" (14). Using the scriptural index, one could create a series of studies from Genesis, Romans, 2 Corinthians, and other books.

2. *Tips for Leaders of Youth Bible Studies* contains an assortment of techniques to make teachers more successful in the classroom and more influential in their students' lives. The material in this section will be new with each book in the series.

3. An *Evaluation form* is included at the end of this book. Your comments and suggestions will help to shape future books in the series and other youth Bible study materials to come. Simply complete the evaluation, fold it, and mail it after you have used a few of the studies in the book.

About the Group Process

The process of group discussion is an important part of these studies. Group discussion, especially if the leader is not directly in control of each group, may be uncomfortable for some at first. A few words may be of assistance.

Physical Arrangements

Almost any physical arrangement will work for limited amounts of small-group discussion. Ideally, a large room is best, with space in which students can form small circles of chairs. Occasionally, a study will work best with tables, such as study 1 in this book, because of the activities involved. Most often tables are not needed.

In a small room, where a class is accustomed to meeting around a table, small groups are still created easily. For a group of 12 students meeting around a pair of six- or eight-foot tables, form small groups by asking the person closest to each corner to back their chair up and allow the person on each side to turn their chairs around to create triads. In a living-room arrangement, have a few large pillows or folding chairs available; place one in front of a couch or two chairs to form small groups. The person on the pillow or chair could be the facilitator. Investigate other possibilities.

Guidelines

A few guidelines for the leader will be helpful to produce both a healthy discussion and the necessary control involved in these studies.

• *Affirm all answers*, even if you can only say, "That's an interesting viewpoint." Affirmation will create a climate in your group that says "sharing is okay"; criticizing or contradicting answers will stifle participation by group members.

• *Silence is golden.* A good answer to a good question is worth waiting for. Thirty seconds or more of silence may be required for a young person to analyze a question and formulate a response (and 30 seconds can seem like a long time). Resist the temptation to rephrase or clarify the question too quickly; it may only cause confusion.

• *Mine the gold!* Some student responses may on the surface seem "off the wall." Responding with "Why do you say that?" or "Please say more about that" will frequently bring helpful insights.

• *Keep a schedule in mind.*

When allowing small-group discussion, announce a time limit ("Take about three minutes to discuss that in your group."), give a warning ("You have about one more minute to complete your responses"); and then proceed, if possible ("Okay, how did Amy's group respond?").

• *Mingle if necessary.* Eavesdrop on groups during the discussion times; encourage them to stay on task; listen for insights worth sharing.

• Remember, *the group participants are your friends.* Don't be afraid of group discussion. Seek the cooperation of the participants. Allow them to assist you in dealing with those persons who are occasionally disruptive.

• *Vary the ways* in which the small groups are formed. Divide participants by gender, month of birth, sports interests or hobbies, where they live, or color of clothes. There are many more possibilities as well.

• *Appoint leaders.* In large classes, or for longer discussions, each small group may need a leader. It can be a young person appointed at random, an older student, or an adult recruited to facilitate the group's work.

• *Be a good listener;* encourage good listening. Nothing will better encourage others to talk.

• *Be prepared.* Your level of comfort in the discussion situation will be greater when you know where the discussion is heading, have answered the questions ahead of time yourself, and know the goal toward which you are working. An interesting, well-prepared plan will eliminate most disruptive behavior.

Making the Most of Your Small Groups

Using a small group to maximum benefit in your Bible studies may involve the use of consistent groups of young people. If the same five to eight young people (this book frequently suggests no more than five) experience the discussion portions of these studies together each week, relationships will develop providing mutual accountability and a secure enviroment in which students can reflect on the Word of God. In settings involving several grade levels, groups should probably consist of no more than two grade levels if possible.

In some settings, small groups will benefit from discussing and agreeing to a Group Covenant that describes how they will relate to each other. This works best if it is not imposed on the group but willingly agreed to. Common elements of Group Covenants include the following:

• Don't put down anyone or their ideas.

• Don't spread personal information shared in the group.

• Let each group member participate at his or her level of comfort.

• Remember one another in prayer.

1 A New Start: Anyone Can Begin Anew

Where We're Heading

It sometimes feels good to start over. We have the freedom to change, to grow, to begin again at any time because of God's grace. Sin mars our life. Our best intentions often fall short of what is truly best. We want to do what is God-pleasing, but . . . (you know the rest of the story). Yet God, through Christ, makes all things new. Again and again God wipes the slate clean, gives us new starts, and empowers us by the Holy Spirit to make wise decisions and choices.

Objectives

By the end of this session participants will

1. identify ways in which God provides them with a new start through Christ;
2. confess the reality of sin in their daily lives;
3. seek God's grace for a new life in the Spirit.

Lesson Outline: A New Start

Lesson Activity	W/S/I*	Approx. Time Needed	Materials Needed
As Students Arrive	W/I	(before class) plus 5 minutes	duplicate Tangram from Student Page
Challenge 1	W	10 minutes	Tangram pieces, Student Page
Challenge 2	S/W	10 minutes	Tangram pieces, Student Page
Scripture Study	S/W	15 minutes	Bibles
Closing Activity	W	15 minutes	

*W = in whole group; S = in small groups; I = individually.

As Students Arrive

The Tangram is a Chinese puzzle incorporating seven specific geometric shapes. No one knows exactly what year it was discovered, but references to it date back to at least 1813 B.C.

Duplicate the square Tangram illustration from the Student Page onto colored paper, enlarged if possible, for each student. Give it to each student as they arrive. Direct them to cut the shapes along the lines. Then encourage them to make different shapes and designs; the only rule is that they must use all the pieces. Challenge them to see how many different, recognizable figures they can make.

Challenge 1

When all students have arrived, direct them to challenge 1 on the Student Page. Read the directions aloud and turn the group loose. Remind students to use all the pieces when making the fish. After giving students a couple of one-minute attempts, show them the outline of the fish. (You may wish to make an enlarged copy.) Let the students complete the fish following the outline.

Then have them complete one or more of the sentence starters on the Student Page. Many of the students may have experienced some frustration as they attempted to make the design. Ask, "How do you feel when you fail?" Give students an opportunity to share their feelings about specific situations when they have either failed or felt like a failure. Then say, "When I showed you the outline of the fish, you had a new beginning. After failing, how did you feel when you had a new chance?"

Many people try to earn God's love and forgiveness. They do good things with the hope that their good works will earn God's favor. Unfortunately, we can never do anything to earn God's love. All our attempts will end in failure.

Have someone read aloud the Scripture passage from Heb. 10:11–12. Then ask, "How does this passage indicate the hopelessness of trying to earn God's love and forgiveness?" (Students will probably identify "day after day"; "again and again"; and "never take away sins.") Then ask, "What hope does the verse give us in spite of our failures?" (Jesus is the Priest who sacrificed Himself for our sins. God offers us His love and forgiveness by grace alone.) Say this clearly to the class: "Jesus forgives us when we fail. He gives us power to live 'new' lives in service to Him. Just as you followed the outline in creating the fish, Jesus Himself is both the outline and the power for lives of faith."

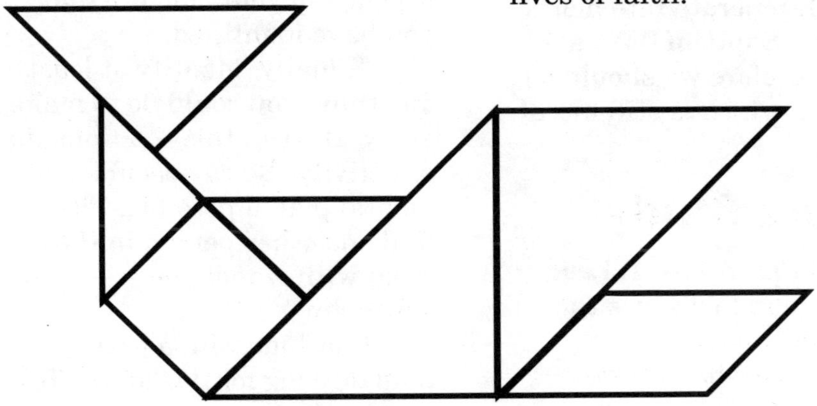

Challenge 2

Challenge the students to use all the Tangram pieces to create a baptismal font in one minute. Before students experience too much frustration, show them the outline of the baptismal font.

After students have successfully made the baptismal font, Read Rom. 6:3–4. Then say, "The symbol of the font reminds us of one of the realities of our loving God. What is that?" (God forgives sin and offers new life through Baptism.) After a few moments, have students complete the sentence starter on their own. Allow volunteers to share their completed sentences.

Keep the focus of the discussion clearly on Christ at work in the Christian through faith (see Gal. 2:20), lest the questions and responses degenerate into moralism based on Baptism ("We are baptized, therefore we should be able to . . . ", which is still moralism).

Scripture Study

Read 2 Cor. 5:17–21. Lead the whole group to discuss the following questions:

1. Who and what are we because of Christ? (A new creation.)

2. What does *reconcile* mean? Why is it emphasized in this passage? (*Reconcile* means to be made God's friend again. Because sin separated us from God, we were His enemies. Yet when He sent Jesus to die in our place, we were reconciled with God—made His friends again.)

Have the students complete one or more of the sentence starters on the Student Page. Give volunteers an opportunity to share their responses.

Closing Activity

Say something like, "At times reconciling the conflicts in our daily life can be a lot like trying to assemble these Tangram puzzles. We have difficulty making things fit.

"Think of a part of your life in which you are experiencing conflict. (With a parent? a brother or sister? a teacher? a friend?) Or think of a part of your life that you'd like to change. (More exercise? a stronger youth group? more regular devotional time?) In other words, where are you looking for a new start?

"Offer a mental prayer of thanks for the new life you have through Christ. Ask His help in the part of your 'old' life that you have identified.

"Finally, identify at least one thing you could do to make a new start in this relationship or activity. Be as specific in your mental plan a possible. Then find one other person in the room with whom you will share your plan."

Conclude with a prayer of thanksgiving for the gift of Christ and for His power in your life and the lives of your students.

A New Start: Anyone Can Begin Anew

2 Corinthians 5:17–21

Challenge 1

Work against the clock to create a fish from Tangram pieces like those in the illustration. You'll have one minute. You must use all the pieces.

Then complete one or more of the following sentence starters.

"When I couldn't make the fish, I felt _________because . . . "

"When I finished making the fish, I felt _________because . . . "

"I feel like a failure when _________ because . . . "

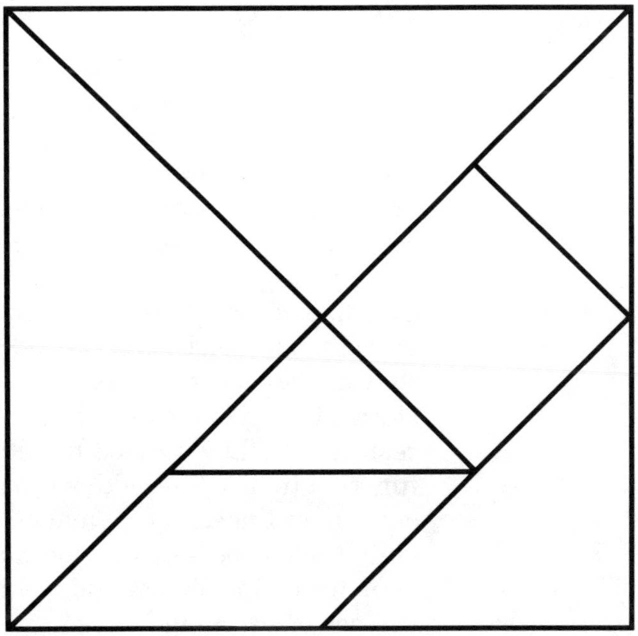

Read Hebrews 10:11–12.

Challenge 2

You're all warmed up. You can do it! Try it again. Use all your Tangram pieces to make a baptismal font.

Then complete the following sentence: "Through my baptism God is at work in me to ________________________________."

Read Romans 6:3–4.

Scripture Study

Faith in Christ enables something special to happen in our lives. It allows us to look at failures as something less than a failure. Check out 2 Corinthians 5:17–21.

Choose one or more of these sentence starters and complete it/them.

"Being made new again means that I . . . "

"The best part about my friendship with God is . . . "

"Becoming an ambassador for Christ means I . . . "

20-2630

2 "Shame on You": A Message You Shouldn't Buy

Where We're Heading

Too often in the lives of young Christians, Law and Gospel are confused. People attempt by means of the Law to accomplish what only the Gospel can achieve. Rather than empowering young people with the message of forgiveness and love through the sacrifice of Jesus, they convey a kind of toxic shame that has devastating results. The Law indeed has its function in any lives—to show us our sin and need for a Savior. Only the Gospel—what God has done for us in Christ Jesus—has the power to change lives.

Objectives

By the end of this session participants will

1. recognize inappropriate messages of shame in their lives and identify appropriate responses to them;
2. enjoy the assurance of daily forgiveness through Christ alone;
3. rejoice confidently as heirs of God's kingdom through faith in Christ Jesus.

Lesson Outline: Shame on You

Lesson Activity	W/S/I*	Approx. Time Needed	Materials Needed
As Students Arrive	W/I	(before class)	chalkboard or newsprint
Shame, Shame, Shame	W	10 minutes	Student Page
Shame Is Nothing New	S/W	15 minutes	Bibles
Shaped by Shame	W	10 minutes	
Our Perfect Parent's Love	S/W	15 minutes	Student Page, Bibles
Closing Activity	W	5 minutes	hymnals or printed confession liturgy

*W = in whole group; S = in small groups; I = individually.

As Students Arrive

Before students arrive write the word *shame* on a sheet of newsprint or on the chalkboard. As students enter the room, greet them. Ask them to either write a definition for shame or write about or illustrate a situation that would cause a person to experience shame. You may have students write on the newsprint, the chalkboard, or on a separate sheet of paper.

When all students have had a chance to do this, have volunteers talk about their responses. Accept all responses at this time without judging them. Ask "how" and "why" questions to help the students think through their responses.

Shame, Shame Shame

Distribute the Student Page. Seek volunteers for or assign the principal parts in the drama. Encourage the students by your own participation to "ham it up."

Then share the following information. "We've all experienced shame. It isn't always bad; shame is a response we feel when we sin. It can motivate us to more positive things.

"However, shame can become poisonous—toxic. Some people can be overwhelmed by shame. It becomes their identity. They see themselves, rather than the sinful actions they commit, as shameful. They lose sight of God's love."

Shame Is Nothing New

Ask the students, "When did people first feel shame?"

Write *Genesis 3:1–13, Jeremiah 31:34, Psalm 103:12,* and these two questions on a chalkboard or on a piece of newsprint.

1. *What in this situation caused shame?*

2. *What keeps our shame from becoming toxic?*

Allow students to work in small groups of 3 to 5 to read the passages and answer the questions. When most groups have finished, have them summarize their answers with the entire class. These are the possible answers.

1. Awareness of their sin caused Adam and Eve to experience shame.

2. God condemns our sinful actions, but offers forgiveness. Through Jesus Christ, shame does not become our identity before God.

Shaped by Shame

Read the following statements for the whole group. Invite them to vote, with thumbs up or thumbs down or another device, on whether the critical statement is likely to induce healthy shame or toxic shame.

1. Kim forgot to bring her algebra book to school. Her teacher says, "I can't believe you did that! (Probably not toxic, if focus is on Kim's action. Kim is not being labeled forgetful.)

2. Jim flunked his algebra test and says, "It's no use; I'll never get this stuff." (Potentially toxic. Jim is accepting a negative view of himself.)

3. Jim's father says, "You're dumb just like your older brother." (Toxic. Focus is on identity.)

4. When Kyle doesn't make the basketball team, her father says, "It must be tough on you to see your friends do better at this than you." (Not toxic. Focus is on a skill, not on Kyle's identity.)

5. Lee forgot to fill up the family car with gas after using it. His mother says, "This is the thanks we get for letting you use the car." (Probably toxic. Lee is labeled as an ungrateful person.)

Our Perfect Father's Love

Say, "The antidote, the remedy, for toxic shame is unconditional love—love like that of a perfect parent. It is love that respects feelings and gives a strong positive, personal identity. It is God's love."

Ask the students in their small groups to look at one of the four Bible passages at the bottom of the Student Page. Make sure each group has a passage. Allow the groups a few minutes to identify the qualities of a loving parent that God, our heavenly Father, portrays. When the groups are finished, ask them to report on their discoveries.

Then ask each student, privately and individually, to write a summary of those passages into an imaginary message from God as He might speak to him or her—parent to child. "What would He say to you? How would He affirm you? What hope would He offer?" (Students could use the back of the Student Page.) This message is only for them; remind them to take it with them if they do not want others to see it.

Closing Activity

Close by reading Psalm 51, in unison or responsively, and conclude with a prayer thanking God for the forgiveness we have through Christ's suffering death, and resurrection.

"Shame on You": A Message You Shouldn't Buy

Genesis 2:22–3:13;
Hebrews 12:1–2

Shame, Shame, Shame

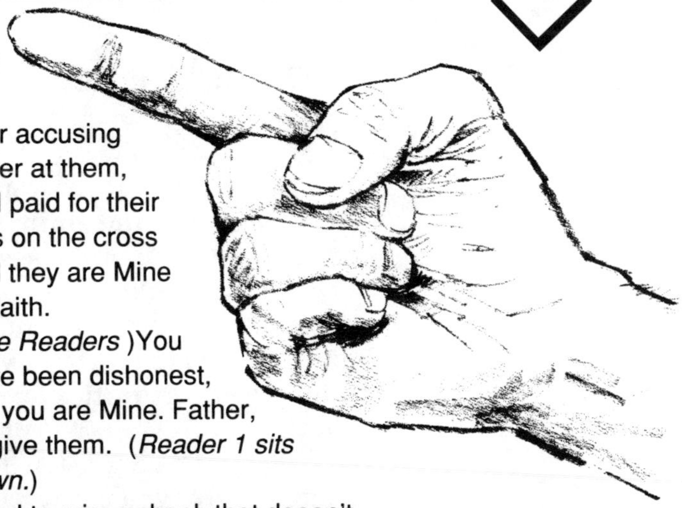

(A Dramatic Reading)

(The first half can be spoken like a chant.)

Satan: Go stand in this corner if you've cheated in school.

Reader 1: I admit it; I did it. I'm a cheat and a fool. (*Reader 1 goes to one corner and faces it.*)

All: Shame! Shame! Shame on you!

Satan: Go stand in that corner if you've lied to miss school.

Reader 2: I admit; I did it. I've lied to skip school. (*Reader 2 goes to a different corner, facing away from the class.*)

All: Shame! Shame! Shame on you!

Satan: Go away to a corner if you've back-talked your folks.

Reader 3: I admit it; I did it. I'm a brat and that's that. (*Reader 3 stands facing a third corner.*)

All: Shame! Shame! Shame on you!

Satan: Stand in a corner if you've taken what doesn't belong to you.

Reader 4: I admit it; I did it. I'm a thief and a crook. (*Reader 4 stands facing the last corner.*)

All: Shame! Shame! Shame on you!

Satan: Go stand in the corner if you've wanted revenge.

Reader 5: They made me angry and irate; all I felt for them was hate. (*Reader 5 searches, can't find a corner, and then sits down in frustration.*)

All: Shame! Shame! Shame on you!

(*After a moment of silence, Jesus speaks conversationally.*)

Jesus: (*to Satan*) Satan, these people are My friends. I paid the price for their sins on a cross. Don't point your accusing finger at them, for I paid for their sins on the cross and they are Mine by faith.

(*To the Readers*)You have been dishonest, but you are Mine. Father, forgive them. (*Reader 1 sits down.*)

You lied to miss school; that doesn't make you a fool. I am the Truth and the Life. (*Reader 2 sits down.*)

You have talked back to your parents, but you are still part of My forgiven family. Remember your Baptism. (*Reader 3 sits down.*)

You have taken what doesn't belong to you, but I proclaim you innocent. Take My body; take My blood—freely given for the forgiveness of all your sins. (*Reader 4 sits down.*)

Yes, you get angry and even hate. Come to Me, all who are burdened with their sin, and I will give you rest for your souls. (*Reader 5 sits down.*)

Satan, get lost! (*Satan sits down.*)

Our Perfect Father's Love

The Bible describes our relationship with God. Summarize the picture of God in the passages below.

Isaiah 49:14–15	Isaiah 61:7–10
Luke 15:21–24	Hebrews 12:1–2

3 Surprise Your Family: Forgive Them!

Where We're Heading

Our sinful nature would deny our faults and sinful behavior. It prevents us from seeking forgiveness. It also leads us to see and to criticize the faults and sins of others in our family and to ignore opportunities for reconciliation.

God in His grace has forgiven us through Christ. He offers us His strength to confront our sins and the sins of others. He empowers us to strengthen our family relationships through forgiveness.

Objectives

By the end of this session participants will

1. describe God's forgiveness at work in Joseph's family;
2. affirm God's forgiveness for themselves;
3. identify areas of need and ways to share that forgiveness with others in their family.

Lesson Outline: Surprise Your Family

Lesson Activity	W/S/I*	Approx. Time Needed	Materials Needed
As Students Arrive	W/I	5 minutes	newsprint or chalkboard, index cards
Family Feud	W/S	15 minutes	Bibles, Student Page
Families Forgive	S	7 minutes	Student Page
We Are Family!	S/W	15 minutes	Student Page
Sharing My Love	I	5 minutes	Student Page
Closing Activity	W	4 minutes	

*W = in whole group; S = in small groups; I = individually.

Opening Activity

Draw a horizontal line on a large sheet of newsprint or butcher paper. Along the line include the following information: 1 = no problem at all; 2 = sort of a problem; 3 = really quite a problem; 4 = terrific problem. Mount it on a bulletin board or the wall.

Give each student an index card. Have participants respond on the card with a number for each of the following situations (lettered A through D) to show how hard this would be for them.

Situation A. Forgiving a brother or sister who embarrassed you in front of other friends at school.

Situation B. Forgiving a parent who punished you unjustly.

Situation C. Forgiving a family member (brother or sister) who put you down in front of your friends.

Situation D. Forgiving yourself when you have wronged a family member.

Allow time for discussion. When all have had a chance to complete the task, ask, "What makes it difficult to forgive family members?"

Family Feud

Direct students to this section on the Student Page. Ask someone to read Gen. 50:15–21 aloud. Ask, "What tension is obvious in the story?" (The brothers were afraid that Joseph would hate them or try to get even with them for their evil actions against him.) Divide your class into small groups of three to five students and ask each group to skim or review the events in Gen. 37:1–34. Ask, "For what reason did the brothers fear Joseph?"

Ask each group to summarize the family history on the lines on the Student Page. Allow several students to share their summaries.

Then ask, "What's the most striking part of this family story?" Invite several responses. Some possible answers are listed below.

- Joseph's brothers' ask for forgiveness.
- Joseph's father urges the brothers to ask for Joseph's forgiveness.
- The brothers send a messenger to ask for forgiveness from Joseph rather than going themselves.
- Joseph cries when he hears the messenger ask for forgiveness.
- Joseph is able to forgive his brothers.

Families Forgive

Now have students work alone to rank the responses in this section. Then have students share their responses in small groups. After students have had time to share, say, "Now I'd like you to think of relationships within your own family."

We Are Family!

In a similar fashion, have students work independently to rank the important needs in their families from one to five. Give students time to share their rankings and the reasons for them in their small groups.

After students have finished this activity, share something along the following lines: "God's love for Joseph enabled him to forgive his brothers in spite of the terrible things they had done to him. God in His love for us sent Jesus to receive the punishment we deserved because of our sin toward Him and others. We don't deserve God's love. Instead, purely out of His grace—His undeserved love—God forgives us through our faith in Jesus. God's love and forgiveness enables us to love and forgive others. We live out God's love for us every time we forgive someone. With our faith strengthened through God's Word and His Sacraments, we are empowered by the Holy Spirit to show concern for our family's welfare. We can refuse to judge the behavior of our family members harshly or unjustly. We can confront wrongs by family members honestly and fairly. We can express our faith in Jesus with our family. And we can forgive members of our family when they have wronged us."

Read, or have a volunteer read, Eph. 6:1–4. Remind the students of God's will for parents and their children. Discuss these questions. "Are parents perfect?" (No, parents too are sinful human beings.) "Why then should we still honor and obey them?" (Because God works through them to bless us, even when that blessing is not immediately clear.) "What is the connection between honor, obedience, and forgiveness?" (Obeying our parents, even when we don't agree with them, shows honor and respect. We honor our parents when we forgive them for their shortcomings as they also forgive us for ours.)

Sharing My Love

Direct the students to this section on the Student Page. Say, "I want you to think of each member of your family. Think of one person in your family who especially needs your love. Jot down a few words or phrases that describe how you might share love with this person." Allow time for volunteers to share.

Closing Activity

Close with a prayer focused on (1) gratitude for God's gift of family; (2) forgiveness for all family members for the times when we fail each other, and when we fail to live up to God's desire and purpose for families; (3) gratitude for the gift of forgiveness and the opportunity to share it with others; and (4) help to love all members of our family.

Surprise Your Family: Forgive Them!

Genesis 50:15–21

Family Feud

Read Genesis 50:15–21. Then skim Genesis 37:1–34 to determine the reason for the tension among family members.

Summarize the family history:

____

____

____

____

____

Families Forgive

The most important message Joseph gave to his brothers was: (Rank in order of importance—1, very important, through 5, least important. Explain your reasoning.)

___ a. "Don't be afraid."
___ b. "Am I in the place of God?"
___ c. "You intended to harm me."
___ d. "But God intended it for good."
___ e. "I will provide for you and your children."

We Are Family!

The most important thing needed in my family is … (Rank the following from 1, most important, to 5, least important, and explain your answers.)

___ a. to show concern for my family's welfare.
___ b. to refuse to judge unjustly or harshly the behavior of family member.
___ c. to confront wrongs honestly and fairly.
___ d. to express my faith in Jesus with my family.
___ e. to forgive members of my family when they have wronged me.

Sharing My Love

One member of my family who especially needs my love is

____

I can demonstrate my love by

____

____

____

____

____

4 Grief: Surviving the Death of Someone You Know

Where We're Heading

Since the fall into sin, death remains a cruel and inescapable reality. Christians believe in the resurrection; yet they grieve when a friend or loved one dies. As we look to Jesus for comfort, as did Mary and Martha at the death of Lazarus, He strengthens us to endure the pain, grow in faith, and face death with hope.

Objectives

By the end of this session participants will

1. describe the stages of grief;
2. share their emotional response to the reality of death;
3. celebrate the hope and confidence that comes from faith in the resurrection.

Lesson Outline: Grief

Lesson Activity	W/S/I*	Approx. Time Needed	Materials Needed
As Students Arrive	W	presession plus 5 minutes	index cards or newsprint and markers
Opening Prayer	W	2 minutes	(in Leaders Guide)
Death: The Last Enemy?	S/W	5 minutes	Student Page
True or False	S/W	10 minutes	Student Page, Bibles
What Scripture Says	W	20 minutes	Bibles (study outline and questions in Leaders Guide)
Stages of Grief	W	10 minutes	Student Page
Closing Activity	W/S	5-15 minutes	index cards or paper and hymnals or newsprint or chalkboard

*W = in whole group; S = in small groups; I = individually.

As Students Arrive

Give each student an index card. Ask them to complete the phrase, "Death is . . . . " Urge them to consider more than one way to complete the phrase. Collect the cards and discuss their responses.

Or . . .

Write with a dark marker "Death is . . . " on a large sheet of newsprint, butcher paper, or poster board. Hang the poster on the wall. Provide markers and urge students to complete the phrase. Give students time to discuss their responses. Accept all responses.

Opening Prayer

Pray aloud the following prayer: "Father, the death of a loved one can be so painful. As we study Your Word this day, help us discover Your healing power for our hurts and words of encouragement for those hurting. We pray in the name of our Lord Jesus, who conquered death and its sting through His death and resurrection. Amen."

Death: The Last Enemy?

Read aloud the quotation from the Student Page. Ask, "Does the statement provide an accurate description of grief?" Urge students in groups of three to five to share personal experiences that support the description. Then have the small groups discuss the printed questions in this section on the Student Page.

True or False

Have students mark the statements concerning death and grief and share them with their small group. Bring them together to discuss their responses and the points below. After each statement is discussed you may read or have a student read the appropriate Bible references.

a. John 11:35—when a Christian dies, we rejoice that through death they have received Christ's victory, but we also miss the dead person.

b. 1 Thess. 4:13—believers mourn or grieve with hope in the victory Jesus proclaimed over death.

c. John 11:35—a person's ability to hold in feelings doesn't indicate strength. Jesus wept over the death of Lazarus.

d. Matt. 5:4—in a moment we will see Jesus deal gently with the anger of Mary and Martha by reminding them of the promise of eternal life for all who believe in Him.

e. There is no predetermined time for grief. Tears and other physical signs of grief eventually give way to less visible grieving.

What Scripture Says

Have volunteers read John 11:17–45 aloud. Then discuss the following questions with the group as a whole:

a. What words of encouragement does Jesus provide to Martha? (John 11:23—"Your brother will rise again.")

b. Why do you think pastors often use the words of Jesus in John 11:25–26 at funerals? (It is a strong affirmation of eternal life.)

c. How does Jesus respond to Mary's grief (John 11:33–35)?

(He grieves with them. Note that Jesus provides comfort to Mary and Martha without judging or denying their grief.)

d. How do Jesus' tears comfort us when we experience the death of a friend or relative? (He is not indifferent. He cares for us too.)

e. How does Jesus' raising Lazarus from the dead comfort us as we mourn? (It demonstrates His power to do the same for us.)

Stages of Grief

Give the following introduction: "Elizabeth Kübler-Ross worked for many years with sick and dying people before writing her classic analysis of grief, *On Death and Dying.* She has identified five emotional stages most people pass through as they deal with personal grief. Knowing these stages can assist us as we experience grief or minister to those experiencing grief. The stages are not all the same length."

Read aloud and discuss the "Stages of Grief" included on the Student Page. Then ask, "How can knowing the stages of grief help you as you experience the death of a loved one?" (You know a little about what to expect.) "How can they help you minister to someone who has recently lost a loved one?" (You can better understand their expressions of grief.) "What indicates that Jesus understood the stages of grief and respected a person's right to experience those stages?" (He grieved with Mary and Martha, crying real tears. He did not deny their grief.)

God has made us His own through our faith in Jesus. He comforts us in all trouble. Read 2 Cor. 1:3–5 aloud. Ask, "What does God empower us to do with the comfort we receive from Him? From whom does the only real comfort come?"

Closing Activities

Give students another index card with the words "Death is . . . " printed on it. Have students complete the phrase again. Ask, "Has your attitude toward death and grief changed since the beginning of this session? If so, how?"

Or . . .

Have students work together or individually to write their own funeral service. Urge them to include Scripture references, hymns, and prayers that comfort those who grieve.

Or . . .

Ask students to roleplay situations in which someone they know has experienced the loss of a friend or family member. Urge students to use one or more of the "Passages of Comfort" from the Student Page.

Or. . .

Invite each participant to choose one of the "Passages of Comfort" from the Student Page. Allow them to share their passage.

Grief: Surviving the Death of Someone You Know

John 11:17–45

Death: The Last Enemy?

In the poem "Death Is the Last Enemy" R. J. St. Clair writes, "If death would only die, we could laugh again." Do you agree?

1. What do you say to people who grieve?
2. Do you think the death of a loved one can ever really die? Why or why not?
3. What do you think? Do people who grieve ever laugh again? Explain your answer.

True or False

______ a. The death of a Christian is a happy occasion.
______ b. If your faith is strong enough, you won't grieve.
______ c. If your faith is strong, you will hold in your feelings.
______ d. Anger during grief is unhealthy and unchristian.
______ e. Grief is okay, but the process should stop after a week or so.

Stages of Grief

Elizabeth Kübler-Ross describes the following stages of grief in her book, *On Death and Dying.*

Stage 1. *Denial.* Denying the existence or reality of death.
Stage 2. *Anger.* "It's not fair!" "Why me, Lord?"
Stage 3. *Bargaining.* We create our own edition of "Let's Make a Deal" with God, ourselves, or other people.
Stage 4. *Depression.* This stage can last a long time and be the most difficult to overcome. A person can lose desire and/or ability to take positive steps to deal with grief in this stage.
Stage 5. *Acceptance.* Not to be confused with agreement. Once we accept the fact that God always deals with us in love and for our own good, hurt becomes bearable.

Passages of Comfort

Job 19:21–27
Psalm 23; 39; 46; 90; 121; 130;139
Isaiah 25:6–9; 61:1–3
Lamentations 3:22–33
John 5:24; 6:37–40; 10:27–29; 14:1–6
Romans 6:3–5; 8:31–39
1 Corinthians 15:1–26, 35–58
1 Thessalonians 4:13–18
1 Peter 1:3–9
1 John 3:1–2
Revelations 7:9–17; 21:2–7

5 Homosexuality: How Should I Respond?

Where We're Heading

Homosexual behavior is sinful. Hating is sinful, too, including hating those who exhibit homosexual behavior. Failure to love those for whom Christ died is sinful. God desires to save all sinners, and He calls us to love them and share both His Law and His Gospel with them. He empowers us for this ministry by Word and Sacrament, which strengthen our faith.

Objectives

By the end of this session participants will

1. confess sinful attitudes toward homosexuals and other sinners;
2. affirm God's redeeming grace in their lives and the lives of others;
3. articulate a biblical response to those who say homosexuality is simply an alternate lifestyle.

Lesson Outline: Homosexuality

Lesson Activity	W/S/I*	Approx. Time Needed	Materials Needed
As Students Arrive	W	5 minutes	chalkboard or index cards
Opening Activity	W	2 minutes	
"What If . . . "	W	13 minutes	Student Page
What Scripture Says	W/S	15 minutes	Bibles, Student Page
Life Application	W	10 minutes	Bibles, Student Page
Closing Activity	W/I	5 minutes	

*W = in whole group; S = in small groups; I = individually.

A Note to the Class Leader

Some of your students may have had a homosexual experience either because of sexual abuse or through experimentation. Some may be attracted to those of the same sex as they struggle with sexual identity. Some may have been "branded" by peers as gay or lesbian because of their mannerisms.

Be aware of this and make every effort to speak God's love and forgiveness sensitively and clearly. Condemn sin but also offer hope and your personal care and concern to any who struggle with this issue. Make it clear that you are open to private conversations on this issue.

As Students Arrive

On a chalkboard or on large index cards, write these words: *butch, fag, fem, queer, homo, gay, alternate lifestyle, homophobia, gay bashing, gay pride.* Ask for students' responses to these words, both positive and negative.

Or . . .

Ask students if they have felt excluded or rejected because they were "different"—in color, abilities, personality, traits, values, etc. Invite students to share their experiences or those of people they know.

Opening Activity

Begin with a prayer like this one: "Heavenly Father, You have created us to love and to receive Your love. But sin has corrupted Your creation, Your creatures, and the way we express love. Open our hearts to be more loving toward those around us, even those who have shut out Your Word. Remind us that when we hate others for what they do, we are guilty of lovelessness. As we remember that Jesus died to redeem all sinners, let us also remember that He calls us to love all people and to share His saving Gospel with them. Empower us for this ministry of grace. Amen."

What If . . .

Direct the students to this exercise on the Student Page. Have students create small groups of three to five and share responses to each situation. After about 10 minutes invite summary statements on each situation from one or more groups. Help students to separate the sinful action from the sinner. God hates sin, but He sent His Son to die for all sinners.

What Scripture Says

Direct your students to this section of the Student Page. Read Rom. 1:24–32 aloud. Discuss the questions on the Student Page with the entire class, or allow students to discuss the questions in small groups. The answers to the questions are as follows: (a) verse 24—sexual impurity, degrading their bodies with one another; v. 25—spiritual lie, worship/service to created things, not to Creator; v. 26—shameful lusts, unnatural relationship; v. 27—inflamed with lusts for same sex, indecent acts, perversion. (b) They abandoned God, so He may abandon them to their sin. (c) Twenty-one

in vv. 24–31 alone. (d) God decrees in Lev. 20:13 that homosexual behavior is punishable by death. Even though people know that God condemns certain behaviors they continue to engage in those behaviors.
(e) Christ died for the ungodly. God's Law shows people their sin and their need for a Savior. The Gospel pronounces His grace and forgiveness to repentant sinners who have faith in Jesus Christ.
(f) In 1 Cor. 6:9–11, Paul implies that some members of the church in Corinth had been male prostitutes—homosexual offenders. Paul ministered to all sinners in Christian love. He knew that sinners could only be changed by the power of the Holy Spirit.

Life Application

Discuss the following questions.

1. As a sinner what do you have in common with a homosexual?

(Homosexual behaviors are sinful and contrary to God's Word. Yet Scripture makes it clear that we all are sinful; we are all under the condemnation of the Law. All sinners need the forgiveness Christ has won for all people through His death and resurrection.)

2. How would Jesus minister to a person imprisoned in an immoral lifestyle?

(Jesus demonstrated compassion, love, and mercy toward people who embraced a lifestyle contrary to God's Word. Direct students to John 8:1–11. Jesus' goal in ministering to the woman is revealed in verse 11—"Go now and leave your life of sin." We minister to homosexual persons inspired by Christ's love for them. We seek to lead them away from their sinful lifestyle by sharing God's Law. By sharing the Gospel we each lead them to a renewed life by grace through faith.)

3. How can a Christian accept a homosexual as a person for whom Christ has died without accepting his or her lifestyle? How can we condemn a person's sinful behavior but love the person enough to share God's Law and Gospel?

(Christians cannot accept homosexual behavior or homosexuality as an alternate lifestyle. But empowered by the Holy Spirit, we can accept a homosexual person as one for whom Christ has died. We share God's condemnation of sin and then share Jesus' forgiveness with the person who is troubled by his or her sin.)

4. What are some practical ways to do this?

(Answers will vary. There may be none; accept that this may continue to be a struggle.)

Closing Activity

Refer to the "What If . . . " activity on the Student Page. Have students roleplay the situations. Remind them to share God's Law and God's Gospel.

Close with a prayer asking God to enable and empower you to love all people.

Homosexuality: How Should I Respond?

Romans 1:24–32

What If . . .

How do you think you would react in the following situations?

- Your favorite cousin shows you pornographic pictures of homosexual activity and admits privately to you of being gay.
- The football coach is fired for making sexual advances toward two players on his team.
- You see your aunt on the evening news, marching in a "gay pride" parade.
- Your favorite teacher is beaten up by some "gay bashers."

What Scripture Says

Read Romans 1:24–32. Then discuss these questions.

a. What are some of the terms used by the apostle Paul to describe sinful sexual be haviors, including homosexuality?

b. What does God threaten for people who rebel against His will again and again?

c. The apostle Paul says that homosexuality leads to other sins. How many other sins does he list?

d. What judgment does God pronounce on those who engage in homosexual activity? (See Leviticus 20:13.)

e. What does God offer to all sinners, including those who have committed sexual sins? (See Romans 5:6–11.)

f. Sometimes it is easy to condemn a person when we don't know them in person. Paul condemns homosexual behavior. But he eagerly shares God's love and grace with sinners who repent. (See 1 Corinthians 6:9–11.) By what power did Paul believe a sinner could be changed?

6 Self-Esteem: Focusing Your "Me-Vision"

Where We're Heading

Young people often have a distorted view of themselves. But devaluing oneself and others is sinful and does not honor God. Healthy self-esteem rests upon the assurance of God's love as revealed in Scripture. God loves each of us personally, intimately, and deeply. He demonstrated this love by creating us and redeeming us through Jesus Christ. His love and forgiveness enable us to offer these same gifts to others.

Objectives

By the end of this session participants will

1. identify positive and negative self-descriptors and sources of influence;
2. consult the Scriptures for an adjusted view of themselves;
3. share a "new view" statement.

Lesson Outline: Focusing Your "Me-Vision"

Lesson Activity	W/S/I*	Approx. Time Needed	Materials Needed
Focus the Picture	I	5 minutes	Student Page, index card
Take a Look	I	10 minutes	(same index card)
Polish the Lens	S/W	15 minutes	Student Page
Try a New Lens	S/W	15 minutes	Bibles, Student Page, newsprint, marker
RePlay the New Vision	I/W	5 minutes	(same index card)
An Extra Idea	W	?	video camera, VCR
Closing Activity	W	2 minutes	

*W = in whole group; S = in small groups ; I = individually.

Focus the Picture

Gather the group together. Organize those present into groups of five to eight. Ask one from each group to facilitate. Make sure everyone has been introduced. Hand out the Student Pages. Also give each student an index card.

Direct the attention of the group to the questions in this section of the Student Page. Invite participants to write 10 words that describe themselves on the index card. Have them do this privately. Do not ask them to share this work.

Take a Look

When most of the students are done, share the following additional instructions.

Say something like, "The words you listed say something about your 'me-vision'—how you see yourself.

"Now mark each word you chose with one or more of the following marks": (Write these marks on newsprint or the chalkboard.)

Mark it:	If it . . .
+	is positive
—	is negative
A	describes activities (ex: writer, athlete, etc.)
R	describes roles you play (ex: daughter, friend)
Q	describes qualities (ex: playful, sincere)
P	describes physical characteristics (ex: tall).

Allow time for this step. Then invite further personal reflection by asking students the following questions:

"Is your list mostly positive or mostly negative?"

"Does it mostly describe activities, roles, qualities, or physical characteristics?"

"What could this indicate about your 'me-vision'?"

This is still an individual activity. No sharing should be required.

Polish the Lens

Direct the students to the sentence stems in this section. Remind them that they will be asked to share at least one of the completed sentences with the others in their small group. When the small groups have finished, invite volunteers to share with the whole group what these activities have taught them about themselves.

Try a New Lens

Direct the groups to this Bible study. Assign two or more passages to each group. Ask students to look up these verses. Have them complete the phrases on the basis of what they read.

Have the groups then discuss each of the questions in this section, reflecting on their Scripture passages. Have a member from each group write responses from their group on newsprint or chalkboard. Review the activity as a large group.

Affirm God's value for each individual as His unique creation. He knows them intimately. His Son has redeemed them. They are called by name and made a member of His family by faith.

Stress the change the Holy Spirit works in us through Word and Sacrament, as they bring us the forgiveness which Christ won for us on the cross. They change our view of God and our view of ouselves. In Christ, I can see myself as a perfect, righteous, forgiven child of God. And in that way, the Holy Spirit motivates and energizes us to respond to God's goodness by valuing others and showing our love for them.

Replay the New Vision

Share the following instructions:

"Complete at least one of the sentence stems. Write it on the other side of your index card from the beginning of our study. Share your response with your small group. Then take it home with you. Put it where you will see it often (a mirror, backpack, etc.) to remind yourself of the new vision that is yours through Jesus Christ, who died for you and rose again." Allow time for the sharing.

An Extra Idea

Use a video camera to tape all or part of the session. Or tape students introducing themselves and reading their new vision statements. Save the tape to show at another class time or review it at the end of class.

Closing Activity

Close with a circle prayer. Invite the students to think about something they like about themselves and to thank God for it. End the prayer with a statement of gratitude to God for the new people you have become through faith in Christ Jesus.

Self–Esteem: Focusing Your "Me-Vision"

Psalm 139:13–14; Romans 3:21–24

Focus the Picture

Pretend you are looking at yourself through the lens of a video camera. What do you see? How would you describe yourself to someone you've never met?

Polish the Lens

Summarize what you've said about yourself by completing these sentences. Plan to share at least one with the group.

Who am I? I am ______________________________

Who influences me? Other people tell me I am ______________

What do I value? I think it is important to ________________

Try a New Lens

Write responses in the columns below using the following Scripture passsages:

Scripture	"God Thinks I Am . . ."	"Because . . ."
Genesis 1:27, 31		
Psalm 139:13–14		
Romans 3:21–24		
Isaiah 43:1		
Galatians 3:26–29		

Discussion questions:

Who does God say I am?

What does God value about me?

How does this view differ from my previous responses?

How can God's view change my view of myself?

How can God's view change my view of other people?

Since God loves and accepts me, what can I offer others?

Replay the New Vision

The Bible says I am

____

Jesus thinks I'm special because

____

Because God loves me, I can

____

I'm not ______________ I'm ______________ in God's eyes!

7 Prejudice: Why Isn't Everyone Like Me?

Where We're Heading

We sin when we reject people because they are different from us or when we diminish the value of any human being by how we treat or think about them. God by His grace has forgiven our sins of prejudice through the life, death, and resurrection of Jesus. Through the working of the Holy Spirit, God has called us into fellowship with one another. He empowers us to value each individual as a gift from God to us.

Objectives

By the end of this session, the participants will

1. challenge previously held assumptions about other cultures and races;
2. identify the value of others who are not like them;
3. celebrate God's action in creating people to be interdependent.

Lesson Outline: Prejudice

Lesson Activity	W/S/I*	Approx. Time Needed	Materials Needed
As Students Arrive	W/I	(before class)	current newspapers
My Personal Definition	W	5 minutes	Student Page
At First Glance	S/W	20 minutes	Student Page, Bibles
Bad News/Good News	W/I	5 minutes	Student Page, Bibles
It Takes All Kinds	W/S	10 minutes	Student Page
Closing Activity	W	5 minutes	

*W = in whole group; S = in small groups; I = individually.

As Students Arrive

Provide news pages from current newspapers. Ask students to find evidence of interpersonal conflict based on racial/cultural prejudice or reports of people from different backgrounds working together to support one another and/or solve common problems. Discuss students' findings.

Or . . .

Ask students to work in pairs to list names of people from various racial/cultural groups who have contributed to the common good of others. Compare lists.

Prejudice: My Personal Definition

Tell students that in today's session they will explore their attitudes about people different from themselves, recognize the value of all kinds of people, and celebrate God's action in making His people one.

Read aloud Rom. 15:7. Ask for volunteers to explain Rom. 15:7 in their own words. Affirm responses that focus on how God gives His people the desire to honor Him in their attitudes and actions toward others.

Then ask students to write a short definition of prejudice. Invite volunteers to share their definitions. A possible definition is "Prejudice is a negative attitude toward others based on limited experience, ignorance, or superficial observation."

Help students recognize that as sinners we often decide all too quickly to reject a person, an idea, or something new to us. Help students see that our self-centeredness leads us to accept those like us and to reject those unlike us.

At First Glance

Direct the students to this section of the Student Page and the cartoon with its statements. Ask them to divide into groups of three to five and to discuss each of the statements in their group, using the questions on the Student Page. Let each group report on one or more of the statements to the whole group. Help the students challenge the assumptions we sometimes make about other cultures and races. As you discuss the questions, talk about the unfairness of stereotyping by virtue of race or cultural background.

Then continue with the paragraph about Peter. You could say, "The apostle Peter was also a product of his culture. There was hatred between Jews and Gentiles." Have volunteers read Acts 10:9–35. Have them compare verses 34–35 to Rom. 15:7. Emphasize the work of the Holy Spirit in the heart and mind of Peter. Note that the Gospel spreads rapidly when cultural barriers break down.

Have students prepare and share their rewording of Acts 10:34–35 in their small group.

Bad News, Good News

This short exercise holds a key to sharing God's power through Christ with the students. Read the "bad news" and then invite each student to look up and explain in their own words the "good news" on the Student Page. Ask for volunteers to share. Then say or rephrase the verse in your own words, "God's action in Jesus has brought us peace, made all who believe in Him one people, broken down walls separating enemies, destroyed sinful hatred through His death on the cross, and reconciled all sinners to God, thereby reconciling sinners to each other.

"For Christ Himself has brought us peace by making Jews and Gentiles, and all of us, one people. With His own body He broke down the wall that separated them and kept them enemies. By His death on the cross Christ destroys our enmity. By means of the cross He unites all races into one body and brings them back to God."

It Takes All Kinds

Ask the students to imagine any kind of band—rock band, jazz band, marching band, or orchestra. Then ask, "What important contribution to the music produced by the band does each of the various instruments make?"

For instance, "In a rock band the drums establish the beat, the lead guitar carries the tune, backup singers fill in harmony, and the keyboard supports the vocals. Each is different and important."

Connect this to human relationships by inviting the small groups to discuss one or both of the challenges in this section of the Student Page. After a few minutes, let each group summarize their discussion for the whole class.

As you hear the responses, stress the power of the Holy Spirit at work in us as God's forgiven people, moving us to love and work together with others as fellow-redeemed people valued by God.

Closing Activities

Close with a prayer, praising God for sending Jesus to be everyone's Brother and for uniting all believers in one family.

If you have additional time, or the opportunity to extend the lesson beyond a single hour, consider one or more of the actitives in the "Celebrate" section below.

Celebrate

1. Plan a "helping hands" project with youth from a congregation culturally different from your own.

Or . . .

2. Prepare a bulletin board for your congregation that illustrates the beauty of diversity in the body of Christ (See 1 Cor. 12:12–21).

Or . . .

3. Identify the cultural/ racial groups represented in your congregation. Do some digging. Find out how individuals from these groups serve together in the life of the church. Write a note from your class, thanking them.

Prejudice: Why Isn't Everyone Like Me?

Acts 10:9–35; Romans 15:7

At First Glance

Read the statements in the cartoon. They are judgments some people may make "at first glance" about different cultures and cultural relationships.

Consider: Why might people make such statements? Are they true? Explain your answers.

The apostle Peter was influenced by his culture (Jewish). He at first rejected people outside his culture (Gentiles). Read Acts 10:9–35 to discover a valuable lesson God taught Peter.

Restate Acts 10:34–35 in your own words.

____

____

Bad News, Good News

The bad news: Sin makes us self-centered. On our own we cannot accept, appreciate, or respect the God-given individuality of others.

The good news: Ephesians 2:14, 16 (Explain these verses in your own words.)

It Takes All Kinds

Discuss one or more of the following with your group:

1. Explain how diversity can be a plus in relationships.
2. Appearances can be deceiving. Tell about a time when your opinion of someone changed once you got to know what was beneath the "outer shell."

8 AIDS: Relating to People with AIDS

Where We're Heading

Disease, pain, and suffering are results of the fall into sin. AIDS can be acquired through sinful, high-risk behavior. But there are "innocent" victims as well. We sin whenever fear, ignorance, and prejudice cloud our service to others. Through His life, death, and resurrection, Christ has forgiven all sins—including those of prejudice and failure to love. As we grow in faith, He enables us to cope with our fears and prejudices and to extend His love to others.

Objectives

By the end of this session, participants will

1. tell how AIDS spreads;
2. face their fears of AIDS and persons with AIDS;
3. describe Christ's response to people who appear as outcasts in His day and in our world today;
4. draw strength from God's Word.

Lesson Outline: AIDS

Lesson Activity	W/S/I*	Approx. Time Needed	Materials Needed
Opening Prayer	W	3 minutes	
Who Acquires the HIV Virus?	W	5 minutes	chalkboard or newsprint, Student Page
My Reactions	W/S	15 minutes	Student Page, chalkboard or newsprint
Exploring God's Word	S/W	20 minutes	Bibles, Student Page
Letter from Todd	I/W	10 minutes	
Closing Activity	W	2 minutes	

*W = in whole group; S = in small groups; I = individually.

As Students Arrive

Explain that in this lesson students will examine their knowledge of AIDS and their feelings about persons with AIDS. They will also explore how they can use the power of God's Word to grow in love and service to people who are hurting.

Lead students in the following prayer: "Dear Father, open our hearts to the power of Your love. Forgive our sins, and by Your Spirit's power, help us use the great opportunities for ministry and compassion that You have placed before us, through Jesus Christ, our Lord. Amen."

Who Can Acquire the HIV Virus?

Ask students to list ways people get AIDS. Write these on a chalkboard or on newsprint. Allow a variety of answers. Then hand out the Student Page. Compare student answers with the section "Who Acquires the HIV Virus?" Point out that HIV is the virus that causes AIDS. Have the students identify and mark the ways AIDS is acquired as the result of sinful behavior.

My Reactions

Direct students to share their feelings about the situations below with four words each. Have them write their responses on the Student Page.

1. A friend dies of AIDS, having received the HIV virus from the contaminated blood he was given 15 years earlier.

2. Your neighbor's son dies of AIDS acquired while living a homosexual lifestyle.

3. Your spouse tests HIV positive after having been unfaithful to you.

After students have written their four words for each item, invite volunteers to share what they have written. Write these on the chalkboard or newsprint.

Help students to analyze their attitude toward persons with AIDS. Stress the power of Christ's forgiveness for each life. Ask, "What are some common fears that people have today about AIDS?" (Close contact with people with AIDS may be one of the fears mentioned. Talk about how we can and can't actually get the disease, etc.) Follow up with "What are some ways that we can overcome these fears?" (Through education, open and mature discussion, avoiding myths and half-truths, relying on the power the Spirit gives through God's Word for the strength to reach out in Christian love and to present a positive witness through God- pleasing behavior, etc.)

Exploring God's Word

Have students work in small groups of three to five. Give them about 10 minutes to discuss the questions. Then review their responses as a whole-group activity. Here are some responses to the questions.

1. All sickness and death entered the world as the result of the fall into sin.

More directly, AIDS is frequently the result of sinful behavior (homosexual relations or drug abuse). No cure has yet been found for AIDS; it always results in death.

2. Jesus desires His power to be displayed. Point out that some become infected with AIDS with no direct connection to sinful actions on their part. Infants are born with the virus. Men and women become infected from unfaithful spouses. People get AIDS from contact with contaminated blood or contaminated blood products.

3. (a.) God desires that everyone receive Jesus' free gift of salvation by grace through faith.

Stress the need for sharing the Law with the unrepentant and the comfort of the Gospel with all who struggle under the burden of sin.

(b.) Jesus welcomes everyone to bring their troubles and burdens to Him. He rejects no repentant person.

Letter from Todd

Say something like, "Let me read you a letter. Imagine that it came from an older cousin of yours who is in college. We'll call him Todd."

"Hey kid, what's up? How is high school these days? College is okay. It's been several months since we've talked, and it will be a while before I'll be able to talk with you in person. I know we haven't been close for quite some time. But there is something that I want to tell you—and it's important. I already told Mom and Dad. I am HIV positive. No joke.

"My test (both times) came back positive. I still can't believe it. I've prayed about this whole situation quite a lot, as you can imagine. I'll be coming home in a week, but please write me now and tell me what you think about this. Like, what is your gut reaction? How are we going to get along when I move back? I really want to know before I see you, so please write soon, okay?

"Hang in there kid, [signed] Todd."

Then say something like, "AIDS has been called 'the leprosy of modern times.' How would you respond to Todd? Write a short reply to him on the back of your Student Page." After allowing time for this, invite volunteers to share their responses. Then ask, "How would Todd be treated when he comes home to your family, friends, or community?" Invite a student to read Matt. 25:38–40 to the group. Say, "As the Spirit of God works through the means of grace in the lives of God's people, we become willing to respond with acts of love toward all people, including people with AIDS." Ask, "What are some ways we can help people with AIDS?"

My Personal Response

Since the disease AIDS is a reality in our world, spend some time also discussing with your class how we can protect ourselves from the virus. God's plan for sexual relations—that they take place between faithful married couples; that those who are not married refrain—offers the best odds by far of staying free of the virus. Under those conditions, the chance of contracting AIDS is extremely small.

Closing Activity

Close with a prayer asking God to provide a cure for AIDS, asking for help to resist any activity through which we risk contracting AIDS, thanking Him for the forgiveness He offers freely through Christ Jesus, and requesting the Spirit's power to help you reach out with God's love to all people. Conclude in Jesus' name.

AIDS: Relating to People with AIDS

John 9:3

Who Can Acquire the HIV Virus?

- Males who engage in homosexual intercourse with someone carrying the HIV virus.
- Intravenous drug users who share needles with an HIV-infected person.
- Males and females who have heterosexual intercourse with persons carrying the HIV virus.
- Hemophiliacs and others who receive blood transfusions and blood products that are HIV-contaminated.
- Infants born to mothers who are HIV-positive.
- Health care professionals who come in contact with the virus.

My Reactions

1. __________ __________ __________ __________
2. __________ __________ __________ __________
3. __________ __________ __________ __________

Exploring God's Word

1. Read Romans 5:12. What is the connection between sin, death, and those with illnesses such as AIDS?

____

2. Not everyone with AIDS acquired the virus through sinful activity. Read John 9:1–3. What does Jesus desire for those who innocently suffer from the results of sin?

____

3. Jesus came to live a perfect life, to die an innocent death, and to rise again to defeat the powers of evil.

a. What does God desire for everyone, including those who became infected with AIDS as the result of sinful activity (1 Tim. 2:4)?

____

b. What does Jesus promise to all who come to Him with the problems and burdens of lives contaminated by sin (John 6:37)?

____

9 Dating: To the Glory of God

Where We're Heading

God created sexuality and sexual desires as part of His divine plan. Through dating, relationships are developed with persons of the opposite sex as a prelude to choosing a marriage partner. God desires that, as in all other relationships, His people honor Him in the way they treat those they date. Where His will has been broken, God freely offers forgiveness, life, and salvation through Jesus atoning work. Through Word and Sacrament, He gives His people the strength to honor Him in their dating relationships.

Objectives

By the end of the session participants will

1. recognize attraction to persons of the opposite sex as God's gift;
2. know that God's forgiveness in Christ covers all sins, no matter how great;
3. identify ways to love and honor those with whom they enter into a dating relationship.

Lesson Outline: Dating

Lesson Activity	W/S/I*	Approx. Time Needed	Materials Needed
Opening Activity	W	5 minutes	chalkboard or newsprint
Josh and Lisa	W	10 minutes	Student Page
God's Words for Us	S/W	20 minutes	Bibles, Student Page
Dating and Alternatives	S/W	15 minutes	newsprint and markers
Closing Activity	W	5 minutes	

*W = in whole group; S = in small groups; I = individually.

As Students Arrive

Write the following words or phrases on newsprint or the chalkboard: *dating; going out; going together; seeing someone.* Ask students to define these terms, explaining how they differ from one another. Invite them to add the terms in use among their peers for these activities. "What do you say to mean that you're interested in only one person? What do you say if you're 'dating' several people?" (For example, common slang at the time this was written suggested "talking" for getting close to a certain person.) Tell the group, "Studies indicate that a significant number of high school students have never been on a date." Let them know that there is nothing wrong with them if they have never dated anyone.

Indicate that today's focus is on God's intention for dating and how the students can honor God as they date.

Pray the following opening prayer: "Dear Lord, thank You for today and the opportunity for us to meet together. Thank You for persons of the opposite sex and the gift of dating. Please send us Your Holy Spirit to help us honor You in all our relationships. In Jesus' name we pray. Amen."

Josh and Lisa

Invite a boy and a girl to read the parts of Josh and Lisa from the Student Page. Or ask students to read the brief script silently.

Discuss, "How do you think Josh feels about Lisa? How do you think Lisa feels about Josh?" (Josh likes Lisa. He wants to ask her out. Lisa told Josh she had other plans and could not go with him to the dance. Perhaps Lisa would like to go out with him at another time. Or maybe she is hinting to Josh that she doesn't want to date him.) If you have time, invite volunteers to improvise the way they think the conversation would go.

Then ask, "What are the benefits of dating?" You could keep track of the answers on the newsprint or chalkboard. (Young people have the opportunity to become better acquainted with persons of the opposite sex and to think about qualities they desire in a marriage partner. It can be an enjoyable activity.)

Follow up with "What harmful or negative things can result from dating?" Write these responses as well. (Persons can be rejected by those they desire to date or have dated; they could sin sexually; or they could become exclusively involved with one person of the opposite sex at the expense of all other relationships.)

God's Words for Us

Direct students' attention to the Bible study. Allow students to work in small groups to answer the questions. Then collect answers from various groups on how each Bible verse relates to dating. The following points can be made during the discussion.

1. (a) God would have us love one another. Love means to always put the best interests of the other person first. Discuss the expression "Love seeks only to give; sex seeks only to get." It is appropriate to make the point that God's plan for dating does not include sexual intercourse.

God has reserved this most intimate expression of oneness for marriage.

(b) God empowers those who belong to Him to be kind and compassionate toward others, ready to forgive others as God in Christ has forgiven us. This includes those who may reject or take advantage of us in any relationship.

(c) In these verses God's people are reminded of the consequences of sexual sin. The Good News contained in these verses is that our bodies are the temple in which the Holy Spirit dwells. Christ has paid the price for us; we belong to Him.

Explain to your students that sexual immorality includes premarital sexual intercourse and actions generated by lust. Students may question, "How far is too far?" (This subject will be covered in greater detail in the study "Sexual Boundaries," *Bible Impact: Book 2.*) Stress the forgiveness that is ours through the blood of Jesus.

(d) Since God lives in us, He gives us the power to honor Him in all we think, say, and do.

(e) Another way we respond to God's goodness to us in Christ is by not causing others to stumble. Discuss ways we can help others honor God in our dating relationships.

2. Trusting in Jesus and His gifts of forgiveness and eternal salvation equips us by the power of the Holy Spirit to love, respect, and forgive others as we develop relationships.

Dating and Alternatives

Move the students back into their small groups with this assignment: "You are a committee assigned the task of preparing a manual for junior high students to prepare them for dating. Prepare a list of five guidelines covering dating behavior and alternatives to dating as a couple. You'll have 10 minutes to write and post your 'Dating Manual.' " Give each group a page or two of newsprint or poster board and a marker. When the time is up, let the class circulate and inspect each other's work. If you have extra time, allow each group to make a brief presentation of their work to the class.

Closing Activity

Close by praying: "Dear Lord, thank You for the gift of dating and for all our satisfying relationships with one another. Please forgive us for Jesus' sake for the mistakes we have made, and help us to forgive ourselves as well as those who have sinned against us. Give us the power to stand firm when we are tempted. Guide us in all our relationships and help us to live Your love in all we think, say, and do. In Jesus' name. Amen."

Dating: To the Glory of God

John 15:12

Josh and Lisa

Josh (*talking on the phone to Lisa*): Hi, Lisa. What's up?
Lisa (*talking on the phone to Josh*): Oh, hi, Josh. Not much. I just got done eating dinner.
Josh: Well, I was wondering if you finished our biology assignment yet.
Lisa: Well, actually I finished it today in study hall. Do you understand how to do it?
Josh: Yes, but I was hoping we could work on it together.
Lisa: Maybe next time.
Josh: Okay. (*Long silence.*) Are you going to the dance Friday night?
Lisa: Yes . . . I was planning on it.
Josh: Would you like to go with me?
Lisa: Well, actually I'm going with a group of my friends, but I'll see you there.
Josh: Sounds good. Talk to you tomorrow in class.
Lisa: Thanks for calling. Bye.

God's Words for Us

1. How do the following verses apply to dating?

a. John 15:12

____

b. Ephesians 4:32

____

c. 1 Corinthians 6:18–20

____

d. 1 Corinthians 10:31

____

e. 1 Corinthians 10:32

____

2. How can the forgiveness and new life and salvation that are yours in Jesus affect your dating life?

____

____

____

10 Risk-Taking: The Myth of Teenage Immortality

Where We're Heading

Whether it stems from the temptation by friends or peers, from the tendency to rebel against authority, or from plain thoughtlessness, teenagers are prone to high-risk behavior. God would not have us test His protection for us nor take it for granted. Neither would He have us treat lightly the gift of life He has given. But God's love is not dependent upon our behavior. He loves us eternally and unconditionally. In Christ He offers forgiveness for all sins. Teens will find help for their emerging self-control in the love of Christ and in the work of the Holy Spirit in their lives.

Objectives

By the end of this session participants will

1. recognize high-risk behavior in their lives and in the lives of others;
2. rejoice in God's care and in the forgiveness and strength for daily living that God offers freely through His Son Jesus;
3. describe ways in which God's protection can be extended through them.

Lesson Outline: Risk-Taking

Lesson Activity	W/S/I*	Approx. Time Needed	Materials Needed
Opening Activity	W	5 minutes	signs
Defining Risky Behavior	I/S/W	20 minutes	Student Page
High-Risk Behaviors in Action	S/W	15 minutes	Student Page, Bibles
David's Response/ Our Response	S/W	10 minutes	Student Page, Bibles
Closing Activity	W/I	5 minutes	

*W = in whole group; S = in small groups; I = individually.

Opening Activity

Before class, make signs that say LOW RISK, MEDIUM RISK, HIGH RISK. Place them on different walls in your room so they can seen by all. Have all teens stand in the middle of the room. Call out an activity or behavior—snow skiing, race car driving, fast/high rides at an amusement park, cheating on a test, sneaking out of the house at night, playing football, riding in a car without seat belts, etc. Direct students to stand under the sign that best describes their feeling about the behavior. Take a few minutes to discuss their choices. Have them return to the middle of the room before calling the next activity or behavior.

Defining Risky Behavior

Organize students into small groups of three to five people. Ask groups to define "high risk." Help students recognize that high-risk behaviors are those that place their welfare in extreme jeopardy.

Refer students to the list on the Student Page. Invite them to rank the items. Allow groups to discuss the list. Discuss their answers as a large group. Accept all responses.

Ask, "When do risky behaviors or activities become sinful?" After students have had an opportunity to respond, say, "Behaviors or activities are sinful when they are contrary to God's Law." You may wish to review the Ten Commandments (Ex. 20:1–17) and have students match the commandment broken with the activity listed on the Student Page. Say, "High-risk behaviors often have negative consequences. What might be some of the consequences of the activities listed on the Student Page?" Allow time for students to respond.

High-Risk Behaviors: A Bible Story

In small groups have students skim 2 Samuel 11. Have groups try to identify at least four high-risk behaviors. You may want to suggest the following Bible verses if students have difficulty finding the behaviors: verse 2, v. 4, v. 15, v. 27. High-risk behaviors included (1) David watching Bathsheba bathing; (2) David sending for Bathsheba even though he knew she was married; (3) David sleeping with Bathsheba; (4) David putting Uriah on the front line; (5) Bathsheba living with David after a short period of mourning.

Ask, "What were the consequences of David's high-risk behavior?" (Uriah was killed and the child that Bathsheba conceived died.)

Have a volunteer read James 1:13–15. Point out the stages of sin. The result of sin is death.

David's Response/ Our Response

Divide the class into small groups. Have students complete the questions on the Student Page. When most have finished, gather the groups together and discuss the answers.

1. David confessed his sin.
2. God forgave David.

3. Through Jesus we can confess our sins to God.

4. God forgives our sins for Jesus' sake.

Say, "God did graciously forgive David for his high-risk, sinful behavior. Unfortunately, David had to live with the consequences of his behavior. As the Holy Spirit strengthens our faith through Word and Sacrament, we can do that which God desires—refraining from sinful, high-risk behaviors or from high-risk behaviors that would lead us to sin."

Challenge

Challenge students to confront a person they might know who is involved in a high-risk behavior. Offer the following suggestions:

1. Find opportunities to speak with that person. If your first talk is unsuccessful, talk to him or her again. If he or she still refuses to listen, bring other concerned friends with you and talk with him or her again.

2. Suggest that he or she talk with your pastor or DCE or a Christian counselor. Don't give up.

3. Pray for that person and entrust him/her to God's care.

Encourage students to use "I" messages such as "I am concerned about you because . . ." Stress that the goal in such a contact is always to share God's love, grace, and forgiveness. Encourage the class to pray for those involved in high-risk behaviors.

Closing Activity

Close with a prayer thanking God for His forgiveness in Christ and asking for the power of the Holy Spirit to direct everyone to those actions and activities that are best for us. Pray for the Spirit's guidance to share God's love through our words and actions toward others. Conclude in Jesus' name.

2 Samuel 11

Risk-Taking: The Myth of Teenage Immortality

Defining Risky Behavior

Below are some activities that some might consider "high risk. " Rank them from 1 to 10—with 1 having the greatest risk and 10 having the least risk.

_______ Drinking alcoholic beverages
_______ Attending a seance "just for fun"
_______ Looking at sexually arousing pictures
_______ Smoking cigarettes
_______ Joining a gang
_______ Overeating
_______ Shoplifting
_______ Mountain climbing
_______ Bungie jumping
_______ Having sex outside of marriage

High-Risk Behaviors in Action: A Bible Story

Skim the story of David and Bathsheba (2 Samuel 11). Identify four high-risk behaviors. Consider: What made the behaviors high risk and what were the results of the behaviors? What made David's high-risk behaviors sinful?

1. ______________________________
2. ______________________________
3. ______________________________
4. ______________________________

Read James 1:13–15. What is the ultimate result of sin?

David's Response/Our Response

1. How did David respond when confronted with his sin? See 2 Samuel 12:13.

____

2. What was God's response to David's confession? See 2 Samuel 12:13.

____

3. How can we respond when confronted with our sin. See 1 John 1:9.

____

4. What is God's response to our confession?

____

____

11 Suicide: Final Exit or the Wrong Door?

Where We're Heading

Lack of faith and misunderstanding God's purpose for life can result in a person accepting suicide as a solution to a life gripped by despair, pain, grief, or hopelessness. A person considering suicide may doubt the reality of eternity or desire relief by escaping the present life to begin life eternal. Sin causes us to ignore God and His purpose for our life and to take matters of life and death into our own hands. God forgives us for values and behaviors tainted by sin and offers us hope in the midst of hopelessness and peace in the wake of despair.

Objectives

By the end of this session the participants will

1. identify the likely circumstances leading young people to consider suicide;
2. affirm their faith in a God who forgives us through Christ and empowers us for lives of productive service to Him;
3. find strength in God's Word for times of despair.

Lesson Outline: Suicide

Lesson Activity	W/S/I*	Approx. Time Needed	Materials Needed
Opening Activity	W/I	10 minutes	
Agree or Disagree	S/I	15 minutes	Student Page
Reasons to Die?	S/W	10 minutes	Student page Newsprint/paper
A Reason to Live	W/S	15 minutes	Student Page Chalkboard/newsprint
Life Application	W/I	5 minutes	Bibles
Closing Activity	W/S	5 minutes	
Optional Activities			Student Page paper, VCR and TV

*W = in whole group; S = in small groups; I = individually.

An Important Note

If at any time in this session a student expresses suicidal thoughts, take it seriously. Let the student know that you are available to listen. Seek appropriate help if the situation warrants.

Opening Activity

Ask the students to respond to the questions below. Allow them to share freely without evaluating their opinions. Say something like, "Think of suicides you have seen on television or in movies. Who was it that committed suicide? How did they do it? What were their reasons? How did the scene make you feel? Do you agree or disagree with what the character did?

"Are you aware of suicide or attempts at it closer to home [friends, classmates, people in your community]? Do you know why they took place? How do you feel about those experiences?"

Agree or Disagree

Ask the students to mark the statements in this section of the Student Page. If space allows, you may designate one side of the room as "agree" and the other as "disagree." Have the students stand on opposite sides of the room to reflect their opinion as you read each statement. Let students share their reasoning. Then add these insights:

1. Many experts would agree that suicide is a symptom of problems in a person's life.

2. Although a single event may be the catalyst, most teen suicides are caused by a combination of factors, and many are the result of prolonged depression.

3. Suicide affects all kinds of people. Students who appear to "have it all together" may be the ones who experience the most pressure. They are not immune to the risk of suicide.

4. Many suicide attempts are cries for help. Even those who believe they truly want to die may have mixed feelings.

5. It is clear that the desire to take one's own life is a sin. But we Christians recognize that we all sin daily. Sin does not erase our Christian faith; rather it points out our need for Jesus Christ as Savior.

Reasons to Die?

If possible, divide your class into two or more groups of three to five students. Ask each group to brainstorm a list of responses to the questions in this part of the Student Page. Give each group a sheet of newsprint or paper to record its lists. Let the groups share their lists.

Ask students to evaluate the items on the list realistically. Ask, "What might be positive ways to deal with the situations or events we have listed?" Stress that suicide must be seen as a serious sin that solves *nothing!*

A Reason to Live

Direct the group to the quotation. Then say, "In the midst of hopelessness and despair, Jesus invites us: 'Come to Me, all you who are weary and burdened, and I will give you rest' (Matt. 11:28). When because of lack of faith we make unwise choices or desire to harm ourselves, we can look to Jesus, who even while dying on a cross interceded on our behalf, 'Father, forgive them.' Through His resurrection Jesus proclaimed victory for us over sin, over death, and over the power of the devil. When in faith we look to Jesus for help, we can be sure that nothing can separate us from His love."

Divide again into groups and assign one of the Scripture sections to each. Write the following questions on a chalkboard or on newsprint:

- What hope is there for someone "afraid of living"?
- Do these verses answer the question "Why did this happen to me?" How do you answer that question from a friend?
- What specific help is our faith in Christ in times of despair?

Give the groups time to discuss the questions using their verses. Then ask them to summarize their verses and the hope they find in them with the whole class.

Emphasize the fact that God does not leave us alone in our faith. He provides pastors and fellow Christians who are there precisely to help us see God's hope in our lives.

Life Application

Reread Rom. 8:37–39. Ask the students to fill in the blanks with situations in their own lives that may cause them to feel depressed or hopeless. Let students share if they wish. Accept all student responses. What seems insignificant to you may be a serious issue for a young person. Reaffirm that we are never without hope in Jesus Christ and that nothing can separate us from His love. Jesus lived, died, and rose to give us reason to to live.

Closing Prayer

As you lead the class in a closing prayer, provide a time of silence for students to pray about their own or others' hopeless situations. Then ask the Lord to give renewed hope in the knowledge that nothing will separate us from His love.

Optional Activities

Have each student choose one of the items they have listed under "Reasons to Die?" and write a letter to an imaginary young person who is experiencing that problem.

Or . . .

Worth It is a 33-minute video available through Concordia Publishing House. Portions of it may be appropriate before or during this study. The whole video provides an in-depth, two-session, follow-up study on suicide. To order call 1-800-325-3040 (video and Study Guide 87-0501).

Or . . .

Is a "Hot Line" available in your area for suicide prevention? Look up and post the number.

Suicide: Final Exit or the Wrong Door?

Romans 8; 2 Corinthians 4

Agree or Disagree

______ 1. Suicide is not the problem. It is a symptom of other problems.
______ 2. Most youth who commit suicide do so in reaction to one bad event such as breaking up or failing a class.
______ 3. Star athletes, honor students, and members of the popular crowd are in less danger of attempting suicide because they have more to live for.
______ 4. Some who attempt suicide don't really want to die.
______ 5. People who think about suicide or attempt to take their own lives aren't really Christian.

Reasons to Die?

What kinds of circumstances might lead someone to commit suicide? Think of situations or events that may lead someone to believe they have a reason to die. Make a list on newsprint or on the back of this page.

A Reason to Live

T. Michael Anthony, in *Suicide: Knowing When Your Teen Is at Risk,* writes, "Suicide is not so much the desire to die as it is the fear of living." Suicide is not really about death. It is about pain and hopelessness.

Read the passages below and share how they offer God's hope in a hopeless situation.

Romans 8:18–25, 31–39 2 Corinthians 4:1, 5–12

Romans 8:37–39

No, in all these things we are more than conquerors through Him who loved us. For I am convinced that neither _______ nor _______, neither _______ nor _______, neither _______ nor _______, nor any _______, neither _______ nor _______, nor anything else in all creation, will be able to separate me from the love of God that is in Christ Jesus my Lord. (Paraphrase)

12 Mormons: What Do They Believe?

Where We're Heading

God clearly reveals Himself in His Word, offering His promise of forgiveness of sins and eternal life through faith in Christ Jesus. Through faith strengthened by the Holy Spirit working through the Word, we can be confident in our Savior and prepared to have discussions about Him with others.

Objectives

By the end of this session the participants will

1. realize that the only reliable source of information about God is what God provides to us in His Word;
2. compare what they believe to some of the beliefs of Mormonism;
3. give thanks for the confidence God gives them to talk with others about their Savior.

Lesson Outline: Mormons

Lesson Activity	W/S/I*	Approx. Time Needed	Materials Needed
OpeningActivity	W	5 minutes	
What Do I Believe?	I/W	10 minutes	Student Page, Apostles' Creed
Mormons: What Do They Believe?	W	15 minutes	
Whom Can You Believe?	S/W	15 minutes	Student Page, Bibles
Put Your Money	I/S	10 minutes	Concordances, Bibles
Closing Activity	W	2 minutes	

*W = in whole group; S = in small groups; I = individually.

Advance Preparation

The closing activities will go more smoothly if you prepare in advance. Plan to bring a few large concordance-type resources—or Bibles with smaller concordances in the back. If you have additional time, mark places where verses on *Scripture, Word, Father, Son, Spirit, believe,* and other key terms are found. If you have access to a computerized concordance, you might even print up lists of verses ahead of time.

Opening Activity

Tell the following story:

"The American Bankers Assocation offers a special 10-day class to teach bank tellers how to identify counterfeit money. Interestingly enough, for the first nine days of the class, no one is shown counterfeit money. Everything they handle and examine is real. Only on the last day of the class is counterfeit money shown to the students. Why do you suppose the counterfeit money is shown only on the last day?"

Then ask, "Why is it important to know what you believe before studying what others believe?" Tell students that in today's session they will first examine what they believe about God and then look at some of the teachings of the Mormons.

Or . . .

Label a large sheet of newsprint with the words *God is . . .* Have students write brief descriptions of God on the newsprint as they arrive.

What Do I Believe?

Have students answer the questions on the Student Page independently. Allow volunteers to share their answers. If time permits, have students compare their answers. Then share the following in your own words:

"Throughout the ages people have asked Christians what they believe and/or have challenged the things that Christians believe. For this reason the Christian church has adopted creeds, or 'I believe' statements, that clearly state the teachings of Holy Scripture."

Review the words of the Apostles' Creed. Help the students compare the "I believe" statements of this creed to the answers they gave to the "What do you believe?" questions.

Mormons: What Do They Believe?

Read aloud the statements about Mormon teachings. Ask, "What is wrong with these statements?" You may wish to provide the following additional information concerning Mormonism:

The Mormon Church is well known in North America. Otherwise known as the Church of Jesus Christ of Latter-day Saints, it was begun by a young man named Joseph Smith. Smith was troubled by the conflicts among various denominations and confused about which church to join.

According to Mormon writings, God appeared to Smith in the year 1820 while he was deep in prayer. God told Smith that all religions of that day were wrong, and that God had chosen him to reveal the true religion to the world. Years later, following several subsequent visions, an angel named Moroni is said to have appeared to Smith and directed him to find and dig up a package of special gold plates written in an ancient Egyptian language. Although Smith could not read the plates, the package also contained a pair of "seer stones" that enabled Smith to read and translate the writing. He published this writing in 1830, calling it *The Book of Mormon.*

Religious persecution against the small cult that Smith founded forced them to migrate from New York to Ohio, and later to Illinois. When Smith was killed, his followers split into two groups. One group followed Smith's son, Joseph Smith, Jr., to Kansas City, Missouri, forming the Reorganized Church of Jesus Christ of Latter Day Saints. The second—and larger—group remained faithful to Smith's teaching and followed Brigham Young to Utah. Today the Mormon Church has a vast agricultural, financial, and genealogical empire.

In *How to Respond to . . . the Cults*, Hubert Beck describes a cult as a religious group that has deviated so significantly from the religious thought and norms that gave it birth as to have become a new and altered stream of faith and life. To the extent that the Mormons have redefined Christian beliefs, this definition seems to apply. Rather than adhering to the traditional pillars of the Christian faith, they have altered them.

Mormons may call themselves Christian, but their teachings are definitely not Christian. Mormons believe that Jesus was only a person. They consider the Trinity a pagan attempt to explain the unexplainable.

While accepting the Holy Bible, Mormons believe the Bible can only be understood in the light of the *Book of Mormon.*

Mormons talk about Christ's death for them, but they also teach "works-righteousness"—the need to perform sufficient good works in order to earn entrance into heaven. Since the Mormon heaven has many levels, ambitious members can receive greater rewards if they perform more good works. No member can ever be assured that he or she has done enough to merit forgiveness of sins and eternal life.

Offer the students an opportunity to ask questions or offer insights about what they have heard.

Whom Can You Believe?

Have the students work in groups of three to five to read the brief statement and Scripture verses and to answer the study questions. After each set of questions, allow volunteers to share responses on behalf of each group. Suggested responses for 2 Tim. 3:15–17: (1) Only Scripture is "able to make you wise for salvation through faith in Christ Jesus." (2) God reveals all that we need to know about Him in Scripture.

Suggested responses for 2 Timothy 4:3–4. (3) Mormonism and all other religions that have turned to human reason instead of God's Word are only myths. (4) Chances are that students have heard about some of the teachings of other cult groups or of satanism. All false teachings are examples of itching ears.

Put Your Money Where Your Mouth Is

Read aloud the paragraph and then have students work independently or in small groups to select verses from Scripture. Your advance preparation will help. (See the note "Advance Preparation.")

Closing Activity

Give students an opportunity to offer sentence prayers of thanksgiving to God for the Bible, for their faith, amd for opportunities to discuss their faith with others.

Mormons: What Do They Believe?

2 Timothy 3:15–17; 4:3–4

What Do I Believe?

How would you respond if someone asked you the following questions?

1. What do you believe about the Bible?
2. What do you believe about God?
3. What do you believe about salvation?

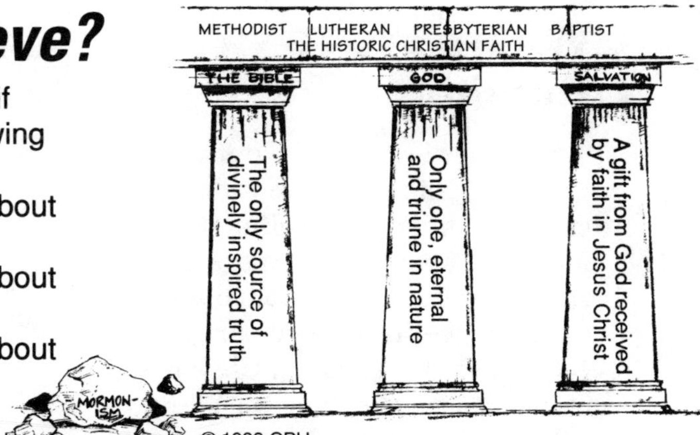

Mormons: What Do They Believe?

The following are teachings taken from official Mormon writings:

1. *The Book of Mormon, The Doctrine and Covenants, The Pearl of Great Price,* and other Mormon writings are accepted as the authoritative Word of God; the Bible is described as incomplete and inaccurately transtated. (*Documentary History of the Church*, Joseph Smith, vol. IV, p. 461)
2. God was once just a man; man can become God. (*Teachings*, Joseph Smith, pp. 345–346)
3. Personal salvation is gained through works of obedience and "celestial marriage". (*Church Education System*, "Achieving a Celestial Marriage", p. 1)

In what ways do these statements contradict our Christian faith?

Whom Can You Believe?

On our own, we can never truly know God. That is why God reveals all we need to know about Him in the Scriptures.

1. Read 2 Timothy 3:15–17. What knowledge of God does Scripture provide us?
2. Why is it so important for us to continue to look to Scripture for questions concerning God?
3. Read 2 Timothy 4:3–4. How does this section describe the teachings of Mormonism and other cults?
4. What other "itching ears" teachings have you heard?

Put Your Money Where Your Mouth Is

Supported by our knowledge of God's Word and faith in His Son, we can talk about our faith in conversation with others. Choose a verse or two of Scripture to support each of the three "pillars of faith." Then take time to learn them so you are ready and able to "*give the reason for the hope that you have*" (1 Peter 3:15).

13 Anger: What Do I Do with My Anger?

Where We're Heading

Anger is real. God built emotions into us at the time of creation. Anger in itself is not bad. What we do with our anger can be sinful. Uncontrolled anger can hurt feelings and destroy relationships. Through Christ, God restores our broken relationshlip with Him, forgives us when we hurt others in our anger, and enables us to use our anger in appropriate ways.

Objectives

By the end of this session the participants will

1. identify things that make them angry;
2. rejoice in God's willingness to overcome His anger over our sin through Christ's death;
3. develop a strategy to deal with anger in a God-pleasing way.

Lesson Outline: Anger

Lesson Activity	W/S/I*	Approx. Time Needed	Materials Needed
As Students Arrive	W/I	(before class)	newspapers
My Anger	W	5 minutes	Student Page, newsprint, and marker
God's Anger	S/I	20 minutes	Student Page, Bibles
How Will I Handle My Anger?	S/W	15 minutes	Student Page, Bibles
My Personal Contract	W/I	5 minutes	Student Page
Closing Activity	W/S	5 minutes	paper and markers

*W = in whole group; S = in small groups; I = individually.

As Students Arrive

Greet each participant as he or she arrives. Direct their attention to newspaper articles you have gathered that relate to anger—crimes, protests, demonstrations, etc. Post the articles on the walls or bulletin boards around the room or give them to students to read and pass along. Informally discuss the articles with students. Ask, "Were the actions appropriate? Have you ever been angry enough to participate in a protest? Have you ever hurt someone out of anger?"

My Anger

Call the class together and distribute copies of the lesson. Direct the students to the "My Anger?" situations on the Student Page. Several suggestions are given. You may want to add students' ideas to this list. Write them on a chalkboard or on a sheet of newsprint. Once you have developed a list of four or five additional items, have the participants choose the situation that makes them most angry and explain the reason for their choice.

Try an "expressive" voting technique—students shaking their fists, growling, or stomping their feet to indicate their choice.

Or ask, "Have you ever 'counted to 10' when you were angry? How far would you have to count if [read the situation]." Tabulate the results. Assure students that anger is okay. Anger is an emotion. What we often do with our anger, however, can make it sinful.

God's Anger

For this activity, it is helpful to have small groups of four to seven students. Instruct each group to read the Scripture references and then discuss the questions that follow. After 15 minutes, or when all small groups are nearly finished, call everyone back together and ask each group to share what they discovered.

Ex. 32:7–10 speaks of God's anger over the sins of the people of Israel. God condemns all sin. (Also see Rom. 6:23.)

Rom. 5:6–11 tells of God's answer to sin. He sent Jesus Christ into this world to suffer and die for all sinners so that they might receive complete forgiveness of sin, including the sinful use of anger. Repentant sinners receive the blessings Christ earned—forgiveness and eternal life.

How Will I Handle My Anger?

Direct the students to the third part of the lesson. Tell them, "God's forgiveness in Christ empowers us to use our anger in God-pleasing ways. In Proverbs, God provided King Solomon with wisdom about anger. Read the following passages and then write some guidelines for anger." Have the students work in small groups or independently. Remind them that through His strengthening of us by Word and Sacrament, the Holy Spirit enables us to control our anger. Possible guidelines would be as follows: "Use gentle words." "Do not let your anger get out of control.

Out-of-control anger causes dissension." "Do not remain angry with a person."

My Personal Contract

Ask the students to complete the personal contract based on the information they have gained from the previous activity. A sample response might be, "With God's help when I get angry I will try to *focus on the situation and not the people involved.*"

Closing Activity

Read Eph. 4:26–27. Then direct the students back into small groups. Ask each group to create a slogan based on these verses or or other passages studied during this session. Sample slogans might include: "Don't go to bed mad" or "Christians need to love one another—that means all the time." Ask each group to share its slogan. Close with a brief prayer and the Lord's Prayer. Point out that as God forgives us we are empowered to forgive others, even those with whom we get angry.

What Do I Do with My Anger?

Exodus 32:7–10;
Romans 5:6–11

My Anger

Choose a situation below that makes you angry, or list one or more of your personal "hot buttons."

- A parent who says no to something I really want to do.
- A friend who knowingly lets me down or disappoints me.
- A teacher who treats me unfairly.
- Seeing other people suffer unjustly.
- Unexpected happenings that interrupt my plans.
- ______________________________
- ______________________________

God's Anger

Exodus 32:7–10

Who is angry?

Why?

Was the anger proper, considering the situation?

Do you think God is angry about your sin? Why or why not?

Romans 5:6–11

Although angry over our sin, what did God do for all people?

Who receives the benefits from God's action? (See John 1:8–9.)

How do we respond to His action on our behalf?

How Will I Handle My Anger?

Read the following passages: Proverbs 15:1, Proverbs 29:11, and Proverbs 29:22.

Then form some guidelines by using the ideas included in the passages.

Guideline 1 ______________________________

Guideline 2 ______________________________

Guideline 3 ______________________________

My Personal Contract

With God's help, when I get angry I will try to . . .

____

____

14 Ecology: Preserving Our Earthly Inheritance

Where We're Heading

As young Christians seek to respond to concerns about the environment and ecology, their idealism is often dimmed by frustration—the task may seem overwhelming and their apparent resources too small. As people empowered by and responding to God's love in Christ, they can employ the resources God has given them and trust in His might to accomplish what seems beyond their ability.

Objectives

By the end of this session, the participants will

1. acknowledge their failure to fulfill the caretaking role God gave people through Adam and Eve;
2. rejoice in the power God has to "do more than we ask or imagine";
3. identify things that are within their ability, as God helps them, to restore and preserve God's creation.

Lesson Outline: Ecology

Lesson Activity	W/S/I*	Approx. Time Needed	Materials Needed
As Students Arrive	W/I	(before class)	newspapers, magazines, paper/pencils, and Bibles
Opening Devotion	W	5 minutes	hymnals
Focusing on the Topic	W	5 minutes	environment statistics (obtained locally)
About the Creation	S/W	15 minutes	Student Page
But How Should I Respond?	S/W	20 minutes	
But What Can I Do?	W	10 minutes	Student Page
If You Have More Time	W/S		trash (paper bags, old Styrofoam cups, manila folders, cereal boxes), tape glue, wire, etc.

*W = in whole group; S = in small groups; I = individually.

Advance Preparation

If possible, find current statistics or news articles about the state of the environment (e.g., endangered species, toxins in the oceans, etc.), or recruit a student to do so. Check with a local library's reference desk or with a school science teacher.

As Students Arrive

Have students cut out magazine and newspaper pictures, ads, and headlines that point to the causes of environmental problems. Display them under the title "Who's Really to Blame?"

Or . . .

Have students list on paper God's actions on each of the six days of creation. Then have the whole class use Gen. 1:1–26 to create a complete summary. Give a prize (a donut, a badge, a free ticket to next month's youth group activity) to the student with the most accurate list.

Opening Devotion

Read Psalm 148, perhaps responsively by whole verses. Sing "All Creatures of Our God and King" or several stanzas of "Earth and All Stars."

Focusing on the Topic

If you have current statistics about the earth's environment, share them in one of these ways:

1. Distribute copies of the statistics or display them. Ask, "Which of these facts do you find most frightening? Which is most surprising? Which would you most like to be able to change?"

2. By class vote, rank the statistics from "most serious or disturbing" to "least serious."

3. Change the statistics into quiz or trivia questions. Divide into teams for a "Quiz Bowl."

If you do not have statistics available, ask students to share information they know about ecology and the environment. Or see what can be learned from the newspapers and magazines used in the "As Students Arrive" activity.

About the Creation

Review Gen. 1:28–31. Distribute the Student Page and pencils. Allow students to discuss their responses to the first section in groups of four to seven. Note that answers will vary. Explain that *subdue* and *rule over* mean "take care of." It is important for students to understand God's will regarding our role in His creation. We often fail in our caretaking role. It is appropriate to recognize how people have failed to meet their God-given responsibility collectively and individually. Discuss how students may have harmed the environment through their actions or their lack of action. Ask, "What products have you used in the past 24 hours that could harm the earth?"

But How Should I Respond?

Ask the students whether they agree with the following statements as you read them to the whole class. Let students give the reason for their answers. After students have had an opportunity to give their opinions, share the insights that follow each statement.

1. "Pouring used motor oil down a sewer is a sin." (Pouring oil down a storm sewer can contaminate drinking water, fish, and other wildlife as it spills into streams and rivers. This is in direct opposition to God's desire that we serve as caretakers of His creation.)

2. "We treat the earth much worse than people did in Bible times." (Covetousness and carelessness with the earth's resources have probably not changed since Bible times. However, our technology and population growth cause our individual actions to have much more serious consequences.)

3. "Christians should boycott businesses that mess up the environment." (Accept all answers. Make sure students can back up their statements and reasons.)

Emphasize that sinful nature causes us at times to fail to do what is right. Praise God that He continues to forgive us for our sinful failures through Jesus. The Holy Spirit empowers us and strengthens us through Word and Sacraments to do what God desires. Help students realize that we desire to do God's will—to "subdue" and "rule over" His creation.

But What Can I Do?

Direct the students' attention to the cartoon on the Student Page. Read aloud the introductory paragraph.

Have the students work in their groups to list things they could do now to stop or repair some of the damage caused to God's earth. Provide each group with a sheet of newsprint and a marker for this task. Have them post their lists around the room and compare the lists.

Remind students that prayer can be a powerful and valuable step. Urge students to write a prayer on the back of their Student Page asking God to empower them to act responsibly toward His earth. Use the prayers for a closing.

If You Have More Time

Invite students to create a trash sculpture titled "Creation." Provide paper bags, newspapers, old Styrofoam cups, manila folders, cereal boxes, and glue, tape, or wire to attach the trash together. Display completed projects in a prominent place.

Ecology: Preserving Our Earthly Inheritance

Genesis 1:28–31; 2:15

About the Creation

1. The two very best things that God created in that first week are __________ and __________.

2. What does the Bible mean when it says, "God saw that it was good"? Mark each correct response.

- Everything was the right color, size, etc.
- It turned out just like He expected it to.
- There was nothing evil in the world.
- Everything was designed to last forever, with no death.
- Everything He saw made Him feel good.
- (Write your own idea here:)

____

3. What did God mean when He told the humans to "subdue" the earth and "rule over" every living creature?

"The problem is too big. I'm just one person. Even if I somehow managed to convince every family in my community to recycle all their paper and cardboard, it wouldn't change the real problems at all."

But What Can I Do?

The problems can seem overwhelming. What can you do about the destruction of the rain forests or the extinction of the panda? By yourself, not much. But watch what happens when you place your abilities and efforts into the hands of the Creator of all things. He redeemed you through Jesus' blood. He continues to strengthen your faith. Amazing things can happen!

Ephesians 3:20 calls God the one "who is able to do immeasurably more than all we ask or imagine." In the Old Testament, Ezra states that God made the heavens, the earth, and everything in them, and still preserves all of them (Nehemiah 9:6). The job of "preserving" the earth is not one that should overwhelm us. Scripture promises that God does it Himself. He takes our efforts, as small as they may seem, and uses them in powerful ways to accomplish His will.

15 Who's to Blame? Isn't God Supposed to Be Fair?

Where We're Heading

Young people usually have a strong sense of justice. When life does not seem fair, they may blame God. Through Jesus He grants forgiveness to repentant sinners for the times when we fail to trust in His promises. The Holy Spirit enables us to depend on God and to confess that He is still at work—supporting His people and accomplishing His plans.

Objectives

By the end of this session, the participants will

1. recognize God's right and ability to judge all things according to His will;
2. rejoice in God's mercy, demonstrated through His only Son's death on a cross for them and for all people;
3. embrace the injustices of this world as lessons to learn and opportunities to serve.

Lesson Outline: Who's to Blame?

Lesson Activity	W/S/I*	Approx. Time Needed	Materials Needed
As Students Arrive	W/I	(before class)	newsprint, markers, crayons, poster board
Opening Activity	W	5 minutes	index cards, newsprint, marker
"That Was Then . . ."	W	15 minutes	Student Page, Bibles
"This Is Now . . ."	S	15 minutes	Bibles, Student Page, ruled paper
"But How Do I . . ."	W/S	5 minutes	Bibles
Closing Activity	I	5 minutes	white construction paper/ poster board

*W = in whole group; S = in small groups; I = individually.

Before Class

Hang two or three pieces of newsprint on a bulletin board, easel, or wall. Label each "It's not fair when . . . " Have markers by each paper. Also, gather a variety of "arts and crafts" materials—markers, crayons, etc.—and heavy white paper or poster board for the closing activity.

As Students Arrive

Ask students to think about situations they've witnessed or experienced that seemed unfair. Ask them to list these situations on the newsprint. Be prepared to offer examples to get them started. Ask, "Why do you think the situation is unfair?"

Opening Activity

Discuss with the class the unfair situations students listed. Create a continuum from 1–10 in the front of the classroom. Explain that students will need to decide how difficult it would be for them to accept each circumstance, without any negative feelings, using a scale of 1–10—1, having little or not trouble accepting, through 10, having a major problem accepting.

Or . . .

Discuss each of the situations the students have listed. As you do so, write each one on a separate index card. When all the situations have been written on cards, add a few "positive" experiences (being named in a rich uncle's will, someone buying you a new car, getting front-row seats at a favorite concert, etc.). Mix these in, shuffle the cards, and then deal one or more to each student. Have students roleplay a possible response to the situation(s) they were dealt.

"That Was Then . . ."

Whenever something seems unfair, we seem able to justify our opinion, blame someone else, or even blame God. Give students a chance to consider each of the people from the Bible and try to explain why each could easily have cried "It's not fair." Seek a volunteer for each. Or if your class is large, allow students to work in small groups. Offer the following Bible references: Adam and Eve's removal from the Garden of Eden (Gen. 3:23), Cain (Gen. 4:3–5), Abel (Gen. 4:8), Esau (Gen. 27:33–36), Joseph (Gen. 37:26), Samson (Judges 14:12–20; 16), Job (Job 1:12–22; 2:6–8), Daniel (Dan. 6:1–16), Paul and Silas (Acts 16:16ff.). Ask, "Which of these individuals do you think had a legitimate reason to say 'It's not fair!'? Which did not? Explain your answer."

"This Is Now . . . "

Say, "That's great for those people, but God worked differently back then. It was probably a lot easier to deal with the hardships and the struggles when God spoke to people directly. But this is today. What do we have to hang on to when life seems so unfair? Where do we begin?"

Read 2 Tim. 3:16. Then say, "God continues to speak directly to us today in His Word. What does God say to us in His Word about struggles and hardships?" Allow time for students to offer suggestions. Then divide the class into small groups and assign each group one or more of the following passages: Job 2:10, Is. 55:8–9, Pro. 3:11–12, Rom. 8:28, 1 Peter 3:17, 1 Cor. 10:24, Heb. 6:17–20, Heb. 10:19–25, Heb. 12:1–11. Have each group paraphrase the main idea of the passage as if the author were talking to people today. Give them five to seven minutes to write their paraphrase. Then have volunteers address the rest of the group as a friend would, in an attempt to encourage or support them with this new-found wisdom.

After students have shared their paraphrase, say, "God's Word offers forgiveness through Jesus for the times we doubt God's activity in our life and for the times we blame Him for our troubles. His love and forgiveness enables us to approach hardships with confidence and hope."

"But How Do I . . . "

Ask, "How can we daily 'let go and let God'?" Check out Heb. 10:23–25 for some practical suggestions.

Give students a few minutes in their small groups to discover the three suggestions. (1) "Hold on to the hope" of salvation through Christ, found in God's Word. (2) "Spur one another on to good deeds" as you work by God's power to correct any unfairness you observe. (3) "Meet together" in worship or "encourage one another" in all circumstances, especially in difficult times.

Emphasize that God's Word is the one source of strength and hope found in each suggestion. God reveals His salvation through Christ only in His Word; God tells how Christians are to treat one another in His Word; and in worship God speaks to us in His Word.

Baptism also has a great deal to offer the person who doubts God's love. As an accomplished fact, it assures us that Christ's death was meant, not just for the whole world, but for me in particular. This is equally true for the Lord's Supper.

Closing Activity

Give each participant a large piece of white construction paper. Using materials available, students are to design a collage or poster with a slogan or other catchy phrase to remind themselves of one of the truths they discovered today. It could be about God's promises to take care of us and work things out, even when we don't understand or it seems unfair. Encourage students to make their project eye-catching and colorful, but not to let their creativity get in the way of the message.

Or . . .

Design an encouraging Christian T-shirt based on this lesson, front only or front and back. What would it say? How about a visual design?

Close by asking about any specific concerns or frustrations that currently plague the participants or someone they know. Include these concerns in prayer.

Who's to Blame? Isn't God Supposed to Be Fair?

Isaiah 55:8; Hebrews 10:23–25

"That Was Then . . . "

You think you've got it bad? Consider the following Bible characters. Pick one and tell why they may have felt unfairly treated.

Adam	**Abel**	**Samson**
Eve	**Esau**	**Job**
Cain	**Joseph**	**Daniel**
		Paul and Silas

"This Is Now . . . "

Dear ____________________, I'd like to try to help . . .

On a separate sheet of paper, write a paragraph or two paraphrasing the hope and encouragement you find in God's Word. Consider one or more of the following Scripture references: Job 2:10, Isaiah 55:8–9, Proverbs 3:11–12, Romans 8:28, 1 Corinthians 10:24, Hebrews 6:17–20, Hebrews 10:19–25, Hebrews 12:1–11, 1 Peter 3:17.

"But How Do I . . . "

God in His mercy has not left us alone to deal with our concerns. In Hebrews 10:23–25 God offers three suggestions by which Christians are strengthened to overcome difficulties—even events that seem unfair.

verse 23 ____

verse 24 ____

verse 25 ____

16 It's My Music: So It's My Decision, Right?

Where We're Heading

Music can be a high-tension issue for young people, perhaps because they see it as a personal expression of "their culture." We sin when we allow outside influences to change the values that flow from our faith in Christ. Music that promotes behavior or attitudes contrary to God's will "corrupts good character" (1 Cor. 15:33). Jesus suffered and died on a cross for the times we turn away from Him and His will for our life. As the Spirit works in us, we can wisely choose that which reflects our faith.

Objectives

By the end of this session, the participants will

1. recognize that music communicates the values of each generation;
2. seek music that promotes values consistent with the Christian faith;
3. boldly express the Christian faith as they choose and defend their choices in music.

Lesson Outline: Music

Lesson Activity	W/S/I*	Approx. Time Needed	Materials Needed
Opening Activity	W/I	10 minutes	
Tune Power	W	15 minutes	Student Page
Don't Blame It All on Rock-n-Roll	W/S	15 minutes	Bibles, index cards Student Page
My Personal Contract	W/I	10 minutes	Student Page
Optional Activity	I	10 minutes	*Billboard* Top 10
Closing Activity	W	5 minutes	Bibles

*W = in whole group; S = in small groups; I = individually.

Opening Activities

How many of the following challenges can your class complete?

• Sing or recite the words to "The Brady Bunch" theme song.

• Sing or recite the words to "Gilligan's Island" theme song.

• Sing or recite the words to "The Flintstones" theme song.

• Hum or whistle the tune to the "Dallas" theme song.

• Hum or whistle the tune to the "Bonanza" theme song.

• Sing or recite the words to "The Beverly Hillbillies" theme song.

Tune Power

Say, "You spent four hours studying for your history test. Now you stare at the test, but the facts you studied seem to be lost. Yet you can recite an entire song that you heard for the first time on the way to school this morning. That's an example of the power of music. Companies—from those that make pickup trucks to those that make perfume—understand the power of music." Have students complete the matching activity. Explain that advertising agencies spend millions of dollars each year to obtain music for their commercials. Advertisers look for two things in theme songs—songs that emotionally "connect" their product with the consumer and songs that bring "memorability" to their product.

Ask, "Why do advertisers spend huge amounts of energy and money on music (especially in television advertising, which is essentially a visual medium)?"

Music can influence our thoughts about perfumes, blue jeans, and headache remedies. To what extent does music influence our values, morals, ideas, and causes?

Read aloud the following quote from Dr. Martin Luther:

"Music is a an outstanding gift of God. . . . I place music next to theology and give it the highest praise. . . . Music has the natural power of stimulating and arousing the souls of men."

Don't Blame It All on Rock-n-Roll

Have volunteers read 1 Peter 5:8–9. Discuss the following questions:

"Peter says that the devil is truly hungry for the hearts and minds of people. How might he use music as an effective tool to influence people?"

"Sin is a reality among all people. How does sin show itself through the lyrics of some music?"

Have students complete and discuss the section found on the Student Page.

Say, "As people for whom God sent His Son to suffer and die on a cross to take away our sins, we want to do as He desires." Read aloud Phil. 4:8–9.

Create index cards with the following titles on them: Contemporary Christian, Country, Rock, Heavy Metal, Rap. If possible, divide the class into small groups of two or three. Have each group answer the following question:

"If you evaluated most music in this style by the qualities Paul gives in Phil. 4:8, what percentage of the music do you think would pass the test? Give examples if possible."

After a few minutes have the small groups report. Ask the rest of the class if they agree or disagree, and have them give reasons.

Describe in your own words God's desires about the music we listen to.

My Personal Contract

Say, "God has redeemed us. Once we were dead in sin; now through faith in Christ, we have power to live renewed lives. In this way God has given us the ability and the responsibility to be choosy about the things that we allow to enter our eyes, ears, hearts, and minds. The music we listen to is our choice. We can turn it up, down, on, or off." Then direct students to complete the contract. Assure them that their response will not be shared with anyone.

Optional Activity

Call your local music store and get a list of *Billboard* magazine's top 10 selling albums. List these titles on newsprint or a chalkboard. Then allow students to give personal critiques of the albums with which they are familiar.

Help the class go a little deeper than "I like that one." Ask, "Are the values promoted in the lyrics mostly positive or negative? Do you agree with the message of the song?"

Closing Activity

Read and discuss Col. 3:15–17. After discussion use these words as a closing benediction or "blessing" upon the students.

Or . . .

Read Psalm 100 together. Begin in a whisper, becoming slightly louder with each verse until the class is shouting.

It's My Music: So It's My Decision, Right?

Philippians 4:8–9; Colossians 3:15–17; 1 Peter 5:8–11

Tune Power

Draw a line from the lyrics to the advertisers they represent. (Can you hear the music in your head?)

Mercury	Like a rock, I was strong as I could be . . .
McDonald's	The touch, the feel, the magic of our lives . . .
Chevy Trucks	You've got the right one, baby . . . uh huh.
Cotton	You deserve a break today, so get up and get . .
Diet Pepsi	All this and the quality of . . .

Don't Blame It All on Rock-n-Roll

Look at the non-Christian themes found in some popular music today and match them with the musical style where you might find this theme most often. (Musical styles can be used more than once.)

The occult

Heavy Metal

Sexual promiscuity after marriage

Country

Pop

Rebellion against authority

Violence as a means of settling disputes

Rap

Use of illicit drugs

Sexual relations prior to marriage

Violence against women

Use of alcohol

Rock

My Personal Contract

As a child of God for whom Christ died,

• I will listen critically to the messages of the music I hear.

• when I don't agree with the values promoted in the music that I listen to, I will

____

• when I hear music with lyrics that are positive and uplifting, I will

____

. . . all of this I will do by the power of the Holy Spirit working through Word and Sacrament.

Tips for Leaders of Youth Bible Studies

Half the challenge of leading youth Bible study, according to those who do it regularly, is the need for relevant, Christ-centered, effective study material. The other half of the challenge is growing in one's ability to teach and lead effectively. While the studies in the Bible Impact Series are intended to fill the first half of the challenge, the material in the Introduction and in this section is intended to meet the second.

Skim this section for ideas that spark your interest. Or read it completely. Either way, you'll be supported in your task of helping young people grow in God's Word.

Begin with the End in Mind

A common complaint among young people is that Bible study is irrelevant and boring. The leader has the opportunity to ensure that every study affects the lives of his or her students. We can help it become relevant and interesting to them. Stated simply, we should begin with the end in mind.

Most Bible studies are composed of several steps. These steps may vary in their titles, but their functions are usually similar. *A hook* is a beginning activity or discussion that gains the attention of the class. It helps the class focus on the topic or on a section of Scripture. *A study* explores the Bible's message and meaning in relation to the topic. Finally, *life application,* which when effectively done, helps students grow and change. They can live life in a different and better way—by God's grace.

Life application is almost always the last section of a study. If time is short, if things get sidetracked, if we run late, the end of the class period usually suffers. Life application is shortened or omitted. This diminishes the effectiveness of the study.

So we "begin with the end in mind," knowing what we hope to accomplish as the Holy Spirit works in the lives of the students. We can then more easily reserve the necessary time so that, even if class time is short, the whole lesson is taught.

Study the end of your lesson plans carefully. Memorize the life-application activities. Know where you're going. Your lessons will be more effective, and your students will be more interested.

Get to Know Your Students

Relevant teaching and good relationships are to some degree a function of your personal knowledge of the students you teach. The more you know about them, the easier the task of helping them grow.

One director of Christian education keeps careful track of birthdays among the young people in his congregation. The week before each birthday, he prays for the individual. He makes contact by phone or in person to extend personal wishes. Consider discussing birthday plans or wishes, giving a small gift, or treating the high school student to an outing for an ice cream sundae and conversation.

Another teacher keeps a spiral notebook with a page for each student who attends her class. Each week after class, she adds notes about each student present that day. What concerns did they seem to have? What new information did they share? What helpful or disruptive actions did she notice? (Use this weekly review to guide your prayers for your students. It may also stimulate occasional phone calls that share thanks for good class participation or to remind students of your support for them.)

Law and Gospel

Teachers of youth Bible study should give careful attention to how the teachings of Law and Gospel are applied in their lessons. Human nature leads quickly from reliance on God's grace to reliance on my ability to keep the Law, to be good enough to merit God's favor.

Scripture teaches that eternal life comes only by God's grace through faith in Christ (Eph. 2:8–9). It comes through the Gospel. Scripture also teaches that the power to live according to the Law comes through the Gospel (Gal. 2:20). It is, as Paul says, "Christ in me." Our power for daily Christian living, not just our salvation, comes as a gracious gift from a loving God through faith in Christ.

Since this is true, we should be wary of lessons that are based on such things as "biblical principles" ("if we would only follow them"), or " more effort" ("we should try harder to . . ."), or "exellent example" ("be more like David, or Paul, or even Christ"), unless those lessons also make clear that the power for such effort comes only through our relationship with Christ. Unless the Christ-connection is clear, we and the youth we teach will always get the message that "It is up to me." That's our human nature; that's moralism.

Teachers seeking more help in this area might obtain *God's No and God's Yes*, © 1973 by CPH, a condensation of the writings of C. F. W. Walther.

Flexibility Is Important

Not just in physical exercise, but also in leading youth Bible study, it pays to stay flexible. Remember that you are teaching *people,* not just *lesson material.*

Study materials could not be written for your class exactly as it will exist every time you meet—even if you were to write it yourself. You must keep your class's size, age, background, and knowledge in mind as you prepare a lesson. This does not imply any lack of worth in the materials. But it makes you, the Bible study leader, a critical element in the lesson.

You are the best judge of the likely response of your class to the suggested activities. And you are capable of finding alternatives that will appeal to your students.

You are the one who is "onsite" during the class. Circumstances may dictate last minute adjustments or wholesale revision of your lesson plan. You can:

- Choose lesson activities

based on your knowledge of the class. (If the activities seem likely to be boring, they probably will be.)

• Keep an activity or two in mind or on hand for unexpected extra time or changes in plans. Successful activities from other lessons can be adapted. Books and magazines full of ideas are readily available.

• Respond to substantive concerns expressed in class. ("That's an important issue. Let's take some time to discuss it right now/at the end of class/next week.")

Resources and Readings

Here are a few items you might wish to explore. Pastors and directors of Christian education frequently receive the resources cited and will probably lend them to you. Addresses are provided in case you wish to write for reprints or for more information.

DCE Directions, the new journal of LEA-TEAM, focused the fall 1992 issue around "Teachers of the Faith" and included articles on "Developing Spirituality in Adolescents" by Susan Volden, "Teaching the Faith in Small Groups" by Stephanie Christensen, and "Faith Maturity" by Marvin Bergman.

Volden suggests that "adolescent spirituality" is not an oxymoron. Rather she points to adolescence as prime time for spiritual development because young people are asking questions about their faith. They are looking for answers and experiences which will provide spiritual growth. Further, Volden makes this point: "The development of adolescent spirituality, if it is to be ultimately fruitful, needs to occur within the context of small peer group experience which is intentional and focused." For groups wishing to implement a Bible study model along these lines, Volden would suggest consistent use of the same small groups of five to eight youth from one or two grade levels.

You can contact *DCE Directions* at 6707 Foliage Court, Rosemount, MN 55068.

Teaching the Faith is a series of new video resources (available from CPH) for improving skills in volunteer teachers. Included are separate courses for teachers of junior high classes and senior high classes. The courses are useful for individual or group study; your church will use them over and over as new teachers are recruited to lead Bible studies. Each course costs $79.95 and comes with a 90-minute video and enough material for a class of five.

Check to see if your church has ordered this resource. Arrange class sessions or take the video home for a few evenings. You'll be sure to grow in your skill in "teaching the faith."

Index (for Books 1–8; Book 1 in Bold Print)
of Topics

of Scripture References

Old Testament